Differentiating for Inclus

Target Ladders:

Visual Perception

Mark Hill

Series editor Kate Ruttle

LDA

Note on safety

When working with children with visual perception differences, the adult is responsible at all times for supervising the child and for ensuring that any resources used with the child are safe and appropriate.

A child with visual perception differences will need significant extra help and oversight to ensure safety. Advice regarding adaptation of the environment should be sought from specialist outreach services. Please note that children with this condition need close supervision in all situations that challenge this condition, such as coming into contact with unfamiliar adults/children, and when transitioning between settings and/or spaces.

The authors and publishers in no way take responsibility for the safety and wellbeing of children with whom this resource is being or has been used.

The contents of this book are intended to serve as a guide for practitioners wishing to support a child with visual perception differences. However, any child for whom you have concerns regarding their vision/visual perception should be referred immediately to an optometrist and/or orthoptist.

Permission to photocopy

Target Ladders: Visual Perception

ISBN: 978-1-85503-592-8

© Mark Hill 2015

Illustration on p. 7 © Alila Medical Media

This edition published 2015

10 9 8 7 6 5 4 3 2 1

Printed in the UK by Page Bros Ltd, Norwich

Designed and typeset by Andy Wilson for Green Desert Ltd

LDA, 2 Gregory Street, Hyde, Cheshire SK14 4HR

www.ldalearning.com

Contents

Closing the gap

Although schools are trying to reduce the number of children on their Special Educational Need (SEN) registers, the array of learning difficulties faced by the children is not changing or diminishing. In many areas, the responsibility for identifying learning difficulties, and supporting the children, is being thrust more onto schools because the external services hitherto available to support identification and remediation are fast disappearing. In most primary schools, the responsibility for tackling children's learning challenges continues to lie with class teachers and Special Educational Needs Co-ordinators (SENCos), many of whom are non-specialists.

The Children and Families Bill (2014) and the 2014 Code of Practice (CoP) for SEN both emphasise the importance of high aspirations for children with SEN. The focus for OFSTED inspections has changed too, from a scrutiny of the attainment of the middle and high achievers to that of the progress made by the children with the lowest attainment. Inspectors are now looking for evidence that schools are working to 'close the gap'. The first step in closing the gap is to identify what learners can already do.

Case study

Isabella struggles to read accurately. She omits words or loses her place when reading down from one line to another. Isabella has little reading stamina, tending to fatigue easily, and often has an adverse reaction to being presented with visually complicated worksheets or pages with lots of text. She benefits from a shared reading of text where the adult reads alternate pages. Where there are illustrations and large amounts of text, a mask is used to reduce the visual field and specifically this is lowered from the top of the page to follow the line (rather than below the line being read).

When she is writing, Isabella still reverses letters and digits such as b, s, 5 and 2 despite regular practice. Often her work will have capital letters such as B in the middle of words. This is a strategy she has learnt to help her as she is unable to remember which way round the lower-case 'b' is written. To overcome this Isabella has a laminated card that has the target letters colour-coded. As she writes independently, she traces over with her pencil, effectively 'picking up' the letters, and transfers the correct orientation to her work immediately.

Isabella becomes overwhelmed when asked to tidy up her table or room and cannot always 'see' what she is looking for. Specific directions such as 'Put the yellow bricks in the blue box' are required to direct her attention and to isolate the items to be cleared within the visual field. Sometimes in school this means that a teacher can write a calculation on the whiteboard and unless this is pointed out specifically to Isabella, she will not be able to find it. During teaching Isabella has found highlighting important text useful.

Isabella sometimes walks into door frames or trips over doorsteps. She often reaches for items on a table and will knock them over. It has been important to de-clutter the immediate environment for Isabella and to show an awareness that she may not notice items that have been placed in positions that she is not expecting.

Whether individual targets are recorded on an Individual Education Plan (IEP), an internal target sheet, a Record of Progress or some other mechanism, the fact remains that these children continue to need small steps targets in order to clarify learning priorities and give the children a sense of achievement when they tick off another target.

The CoP stresses the importance of teachers having a good understanding of individual SENs and of using their best endeavours to ensure that a child with SEN gets the support they need. The *Target Ladders* titles focus on one SEN at a time, in order that the range of difficulties and challenges facing young people with that SEN can be acknowledged. If any child in your care has any of the behaviours or difficulties addressed by a book in this series, then the targets listed in that book should be helpful and appropriate whether or not the child has any diagnosis.

The *Target Ladders* books aim to support you in the following ways:

- focusing on what a child *can* do, rather than what they cannot do, in order to identify next steps;
- presenting 'small steps' targets for children;
- suggesting strategies and activities you may find helpful in order to achieve the targets;
- giving you the information you need to use your professional judgement and understanding of the child in determining priorities for learning;
- recognising that every child is different and will follow their own pathway through the targets;
- giving you an overview of the range of differences/difficulties experienced by children with a particular SEN. Not all children will experience all of the differences/difficulties, but once you know and understand the implications of the SEN, it gives you a better understanding as to a child's learning priorities;
- providing a system for setting and monitoring targets which can replace or complement IEPs.

Setting useful targets for a child can be tricky. But '*I can't understand why the high-frequency words are so hard for her*' is not a constructive statement when deciding what the next steps should be. In order to support the child, you need to find out first what they can do already and then break down the next steps.

You are then in a good position to set targets and consider interventions.

Case study

Joseph has an amazing 'eye for detail'. He will remember where items can be found and can always be relied upon to know exactly where the smallest of items belong. However, this does mean that reading books and worksheets can present a problem due to their visual complexity. Joseph has struggled to learn to read. He cannot sustain attention to read along a line of text without being distracted by the busy illustrations or large blocks of text in the book he is reading. He will often read a word, beginning the word with the letter/s from the end of the previous word as he struggles to notice the spaces. Joe has been supported by reducing the visual field and clutter. When reading, where possible, opposite pages are masked and, counterintuitively, once he has had an opportunity to look at and discuss illustrations these are sometimes also masked to avoid the visual distraction.

Joseph is eight years old and is only just beginning to write. He struggles to remember the sequence of movements to create letters or simply to remember the shape of the letters. His lack of discrimination means that he sometimes substitutes a letter for one that is similar. However, his verbal spelling is very good. He has always found drawing particularly difficult. When he copied a building he struggled to see how the simple drawing was connected and so windows were outside of the main building and the roof was disconnected. Recent work on shape symmetry and rotation was particularly difficult for Joseph. Joseph has benefitted from a paired drawing strategy where he is able to copy as the adult draws and explains how to organise the constituent parts of the image.

Although he has this particular eye for detail, he struggled to see and orientate speech marks when completing a piece of work on punctuation. Worksheets are therefore enlarged. Colour coding and highlighting are used to clearly demarcate punctuation or important key information in texts or in cluttered images.

Joseph finds difficulty organising his writing on the page. He appears unable to see how letter sizes relate to one another and cannot write on the lines in his book. Joe has used a combination of sensory paper, where raised lines allow him to 'feel' where the writing sits, and spaced or squared paper that allows him a visual reference for the placement of letters. Joe has also experienced success from regular over-writing of adult lettering and sentences so that his kinaesthetic sense supports and compensates for his visual difficulties.

Using the *Target Ladders* books will enable both non-specialist teachers and SENCos to identify appropriate learning goals for independent learning, to adapt the suggested strategies or ideas for their own pupils, and to begin to impact on children's visual perception needs in order to close the gap between these children and their peers.

What is visual perception?

Light enters our eyes and is picked up by the retina. This visual neural information is then translated via the optic nerve to the visual cortex in the brain for interpretation.

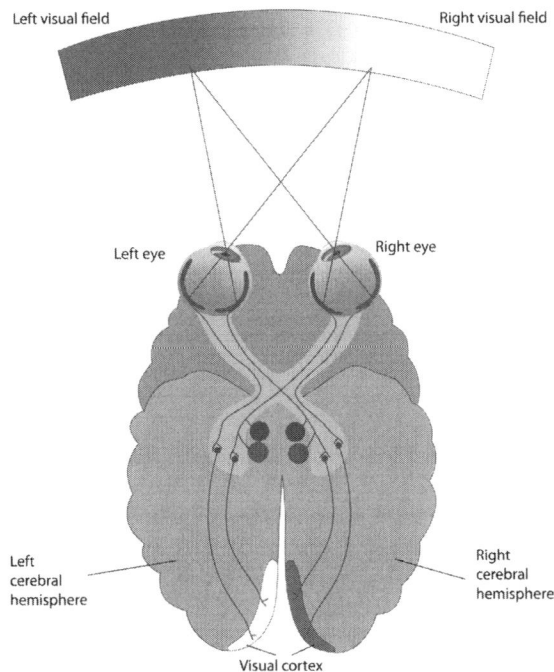

Fig. 1: The visual projection pathway
© Alila Medical Media

Visual perception is the term used to describe the way in which the brain processes visual information. Differences in visual perception are not 'structural differences', so are not related to being long- or short-sighted, but differences in the way visual information is perceived, processed, organised and understood.

We gain meaning from our environment through our visual sense. We learn to process and gain meaning about concepts such as colour, shape and distance. This enables us to both understand and interpret our world and to act upon it. Without the ability to process visual information efficiently and effectively we have difficulty learning and establishing these concepts or even simply functioning within our daily lives. With these skills in deficit, our world becomes confusing and difficult to navigate.

During the early years we develop concepts by engaging with the world around us. Let us take a cup as an example. It is difficult to understand what a cup is without being able to perceive effectively the colour of cups or being able to process the shape and size of cups. These concepts need to be integrated to form a whole, rather than the item being processed as single parts ('handle', 'receptacle' and so on). This ability to perceive effectively means that, even though Cup A may look taller and slimmer or be made of a different material to Cup B, it would still be perceived as a cup. Intact spatial awareness and depth perception would also be necessary to allow you to judge the distance of the cup, so that the cup is not knocked over as you reach for it.

Beyond this, visual perception skills that are unreliable make learning incredibly difficult. We rely on our visual perception to help us differentiate between letters and between words. This in turn allows us to read. We require the ability to perceive spaces between words and to 'fill in' the visual gaps as we skim-read, allowing us to make sense of what we are reading. We rely heavily on the skill of visual perception to recognise and learn to spell words. We require spatial awareness to help us place and space writing accurately, and complex visual sequencing and memory skills to recall and organise what we are copying and writing and even drawing.

Children who experience differences in visual perception are generally accepted to have some, or a combination, of the following difficulties in the underlying sub-skills:

- they may struggle to remember information presented visually;
- they may have difficulty remembering the order of things they have seen;
- they may not recognise people and objects when they have only partially seen them;
- they may not notice either big or small differences between objects or between people;
- they may struggle to understand that an object is still the same object when viewed from different perspectives;
- they may struggle to notice something in a busy background, or may pick out irrelevant details;
- they may have difficulties organising themselves and their materials in space;
- they may appear to be clumsy.

Visual perception skills and their definitions

Visual perception processes are generally divided into a number of sub-skills, which are listed below. It is important to be mindful that visual perception is a complex process involving the interplay of a number of complicated elements. It would be difficult to isolate any one of these skills from the interplay with others, and therefore the areas identified below should not be thought of in isolation:

- visual memory skills;
- visual sequential memory;
- visual closure;
- visual discrimination;
- visual form constancy;
- visual figure ground;
- visual motor integration.

Visual memory skills

Visual/spatial memory is the process whereby a child will recall aspects of the visual environment including objects, their position in space, their features and information relating to those features. It allows the child to recognise their position in space and gives them a sense of left and right, foreground, middle ground and background. This visual process may impact on the child's daily living and curriculum access in some of the following ways:

- recalling objects;
- remembering where items are placed;
- organising the self in the environment;
- organising and orientating objects in relation to the self in the environment;
- understanding left and right;
- orientating letters and digits correctly;
- learning and applying spatial concepts and vocabulary;
- recalling information about objects, people and places;
- traversing spaces safely and efficiently;
- being accurate in physical activities;
- using pencil and paper activity skills.

Visual sequential memory

Visual sequential memory is the process whereby a child will recall sequential aspects of their environment. They will be able to recall items presented in serial order and their serial position. For example, if a child watched a suitcase being packed, they would be able to recall the items placed in the suitcase and the order in which they were placed in the suitcase. This is a very important aspect of visual processing and may impact on the child in terms of daily living and curriculum access in some of the following ways:

- recalling how letters and digits are formed – the sequence of movements – when children are shown how to write;
- drawing and model-making;
- recalling processes in Numeracy;
- recalling number sentences;
- remembering numbers/letters and their sequence;
- reading;
- recalling and constructing appropriately sequenced narratives;
- recalling daily life sequences such as dressing and toileting;
- writing skills and copying written material;
- following instructions from the teaching space;
- spelling skills (that is, the recall of letter order).

Visual closure

Visual closure is the process whereby a child is able to predict visual information from parts, and to complete incomplete visual information. This skill allows a child to scan visual information quickly and 'fill in the gaps' without having to spend time processing every small aspect of the items. For example, this skill allows us to predict 'wind_w' as the word *window*. This important aspect of visual processing may impact both daily living skills and curriculum access because it affects the child's ability to:

- imagine the whole from parts, for example, how to achieve something from a sequence of instructions;
- skim-read;
- complete fun pencil activities such as dot-to-dots;
- predict what an object or item is when part of it is missing or hidden behind something else.

Visual discrimination

Visual discrimination is the ability to identify differences and similarities between objects, people and the environment. It is an essential skill in being able to recognise items and objects but also allows the child to identify features that have been added, removed or changed in some way. This important aspect of visual processing may impact on daily living skills and curriculum access in a variety of ways because it affects the child's:

- sorting skills;
- matching skills;
- classification skills;
- ability to describe;
- development of concepts;
- ability to apply concepts of similarity and difference, which allows the child to organise equipment, materials and the self;
- ability to identify changes to people;
- sense of 'the odd one out';
- ability to identify differences between letters and words.

Visual form constancy

Visual form constancy is the process whereby the child is able to recognise that an item is the same no matter how it is presented. It allows the child to sort objects despite changes to colour, texture, size, orientation, position or environment. This important aspect of visual processing may impact in terms of daily living skills and curriculum access in a variety of ways by affecting the child's:

- ability to recognise known objects;
- ability to distinguish similar objects from the same category (e.g. a pen is still a pen despite changes in colour);
- ability to recognise letters in different fonts, sizes and colours;
- ability to discriminate between words that look similar;
- ability to recognise people encountered in different places;
- understanding that the child's belongings are the same although they may have been moved on their table;
- ability to recognise 2D shapes consistently (e.g. recognising a right-angled triangle although it has been turned upside down).

Visual figure ground

Visual figure ground is the process by which the child is able to locate and isolate specific information and items in a busy background. It allows the individual to identify important and relevant information, rather than be confused and managed by their environment. This skill requires an ability to focus on relevant items and sift out irrelevant information. This important aspect of visual processing may impact in terms of daily living skills and curriculum access in regard to:

- locating specific information on worksheets;
- filtering distractions;
- developing organisational skills;
- isolating individual people and items within a busy environment;
- copying relevant information from the whiteboard and teaching space;
- finding items in pictures;
- locating items in displays;
- establishing a focus on a specific aspect of a task;
- keeping their place in passages of text or when writing;
- locating words on a page.

Visual motor integration

Visual motor integration is the process whereby the child's eyes and hands work together. Our brain processes visual information and assimilates this information in order to organise both fine and gross motor output skills. Sometimes visual motor integration is referred to as 'hand–eye co-ordination'. This important aspect of visual processing may impact in terms of daily living skills and curriculum access in regard to:

- starting and stopping movement;
- picking things up without knocking them over;
- understanding left/right orientation;
- throwing, catching and kicking balls or manipulating other PE equipment;
- developing good handwriting and drawing skills;
- writing on lines, knowing where to write or staying in spaces;
- writing at speed;
- copying from the whiteboard;
- dressing.

Supporting children with visual perception differences

Children with a wide variety of SENs and disabilities may have some degree of difference with their visual perception skills. This means that both daily life skills, such as doing up shoes and coats, and curriculum access can present as major obstacles. Therefore, these children will have to work twice as hard as their peers just to manage their typical day and it is likely that they will become easily fatigued, distracted, anxious and stressed.

Pupils with visual perception differences may require additional adaptations and adjustments to be made in order to support their access to your environment, routines and curriculum. These may include:

- consideration of risk assessment (for example, a child who has a significant depth perception difference may require adaptations to make ascending and descending busy staircases safe);
- adaptations to the general school environment (e.g. step edges made more obvious);
- adaptations to their immediate environment (e.g. preferential seating arrangements);
- adaptations to materials presented for learning (e.g. worksheets simplified);
- adaptations to teaching equipment (e.g. computer desktop changes);
- additional time to complete activities and tasks;
- support from adults and peers;
- adaptations to routines, particularly those involving moving around the environment.

Irlen Syndrome/Scotopic Syndrome

Irlen Syndrome or Scotopic Syndrome is a visual perception dysfunction and is sometimes described as a visual stress. It affects the way an individual's brain interprets and processes the information taken in by the senses.

Individuals experiencing these difficulties are often treated with coloured overlays for their work or with glasses fitted with tinted lenses. These coloured overlays and glasses are individually prescribed for the child, as the colours needed by individuals tend to vary. Therefore, where one child may require amber lenses another may require blue.

Symptoms of Irlen/Scotopic Syndrome may include:

- headaches;
- visual fatigue;
- lack of motivation for school work;
- clumsiness;
- poor concentration;
- poor comprehension;
- complaints about printed text moving, difficulty 'seeing' spaces between words, and losing place on the line and between lines.

Prosopagnosia

Prosopagnosia is a type of face blindness. This term does not mean that the child 'cannot see faces', merely that they may have difficulty with one or more of the following:

- gaining meaning from faces;
- recognising faces;
- matching faces to names;
- recognising emotions;
- remembering people from specific places;
- remembering known people in different places.

Prosopagnosia may be acquired or developmental. Many pupils may not know they have this, as they do not know any differently; they learn to recognise others by smell, or by hairstyle, jewellery or even clothing.

Case study

Bella is almost completely face blind and this seems to vary depending on her level of anxiety. In Reception class she would have to re-learn the faces and connect to the names of class members after each weekend break. Mum found Bella hiding under a computer trolley at the rear of the classroom because 'I couldn't remember anyone'. She would find her own belongings from the cloakroom at the end of the day by using her sense of smell. Finding waiting parents in a busy playground at the end of the day was always very difficult.

She is still often confused by close family relatives, not remembering their names or even if she has seen them before. Bella often asks her Mum and Dad if they are her parents when she is in public places, as it is easy for her to become confused. This is especially the case if Mum has changed her hairstyle or if her parents are doing something that is not typical. For example, on one occasion Mum was carrying boxes in the supermarket (which is something she seldom did) and so Bella thought that she was unlikely to be Mum.

Bella benefited from the opportunity to sit with familiar peers in order to over-learn their names and faces. Class teachers had to be mindful that Bella would not easily be able to find friends on the playground or find a named partner in a large group. It was therefore important for parents and known adults to wear clothing that was bright and easily distinguishable for ease of identification. At the end of the school day it was easier for Bella to be collected from the classroom specifically by parents, or to leave school early, so that she did not have to find her parents in a sea of other parents.

Symptoms of prosopagnosia

- Constant reference to peers as '*he/she/them/they*' (that is, empty reference).
- Shyness even with familiar people.
- Difficulties maintaining and establishing friendships.
- Running to the wrong person.
- Seemingly mistaking an unfamiliar person for someone familiar, based on a simple and quick impression. For example, '*it must be grandad because that person has grey hair*' or '*that must be my cousin because he has a baseball cap on*'.
- Exhibiting distress if significant adults change their hairstyle, clothing or perfume/deodorant.
- Seeming to become unusually attached to or fixated on an individual.
- Avoiding busy places.
- Showing inexplicable anxiety and panic.

Simple strategies to help

- Be aware of the child's great vulnerability in regard to 'stranger danger'.
- Avoid regular changes to your clothing, perfume, deodorant and hairstyle.
- Wear something memorable, especially if you will be in a busy place.
- Avoid regular changes to classroom seating plans. Keep pupils in predictable places where possible.
- Teach the child to repeat names of peers as they are introduced, to support memory.
- Label backs of chairs.
- Create class name badges.
- Play face recognition games, for example, in I Spy style.

Autistic Spectrum

Many adults with autism describe a range of sensory differences including the following:

- fragmented perception, in which only parts are processed. In this case a person may get lost easily as they only process parts of the journey;
- delayed perception, in which they experience an object in parts and then take time to process to the whole;
- distorted perception, in which rooms seem larger or smaller than they really are, or individuals may describe seeing 'in 2D'.

Many conditions such as autism may have associated visual perception differences. While the scope of this book does not allow this topic to be covered in detail, it is essential that all practitioners are mindful that visual perception differences are not only attributable to acquired brain trauma.

Visual perception checklist

Creating a classroom and learning environment that meets the needs of individuals with visual perception differences requires a range of teaching materials and activities. A table of suggestions for teaching and learning materials or activities have been included on the CD. These have been organised alongside their potential uses.

It is not always easy to identify children with visual perception differences and some children may have learnt strategies to overcome their difficulties, thereby potentially masking or reducing their symptoms. To help identify children who may be experiencing visual perception differences a checklist has been included below. The checklist is divided into sections centring on different kinds of difficulties experienced by these children.

This list is not intended to be used as a formal Specialist Assessment tool. Instead it is a list of indicators of visual perception differences to focus your understanding on the types of difficulties faced by children with these challenges across the curriculum, as well as in their self-esteem and behaviour.

Although this is not intended to be used as a screening tool, if you teach a child for whom you would answer *'yes, when compared to the majority of children of the same age'* to most of the questions and/or if you have concerns about the child's visual wellbeing, it would be wise to seek further advice from an occupational therapist or sensory/visual specialist.

Additionally, the checklist would also be a useful tool in order to identify key information that needs to be communicated between staff in your setting. Many aspects of visual perception differences would put the child at a substantial disadvantage in relation to their peers and would certainly, if not accounted for, constitute a safety risk. Information about a child's visual perception differences and needs would need to be included in a Single Page Profile for the child.

VISUAL PERCEPTION PRESENTATION	Yes
Visual memory	
Does the child have difficulty remembering object names?	
Does the child have difficulty remembering where things are in the classroom?	
Does the child lose things/have difficulty remembering position of objects?	
Does the child have difficulties with recall of detail, such as remembering what something/someone looked like?	
Does the child have difficulties recognising when shapes are connected when drawing and connecting these shapes?	

15

Does the child have difficulties recognising when shapes appear within other shapes in drawing?	
Does the child forget something they have seen before (e.g. they read a word on one line but forget it by the line below)?	
Does the child have difficulty copying from the whiteboard?	

Depth perception

Does the child trip over objects and furniture?	
Does the child walk into people without moving from their path in time?	
Does the child bump into door frames and furniture?	
Does the child appear clumsy and knock things over (e.g. water pots on the table in art sessions, or pencil pots)?	
Does the child hold onto peers when attempting to find a place to sit?	
Does the child complain about seeing in 2D?	
Does the child complain about the footpath falling away as they walk?	
Does the child appear to feel that the room is a different size from its real dimensions?	
Does the child appear unsure when stepping down from PE apparatus?	
Does the child appear unsure when ascending and descending stairs (i.e. holds onto hand rail with two hands)?	

Visual sequential memory

Does the child have difficulties recalling information copied from the board?	
Does the child have difficulties recalling letter patterns (e.g. *igh*) in the correct order?	
Does the child have difficulties learning and retaining high-frequency words?	
Does the child have difficulties recalling and following sequences and processes (e.g. following calculations such as 2+3=5)?	
Does the child have difficulties recalling sequences of movement to create letters/digits/shapes and so on?	
Does the child get lost, because they are unable to remember key features on a route?	

Visual closure

Does the child have difficulty recognising a word from its constituent parts?	
Does the child have difficulty understanding, recognising and working with fractions and percentages?	
Does the child have difficulty forming letters properly?	
Does the child become confused following and interpreting mathematical calculations?	
Does the child have difficulties putting letters together to make words (e.g. c-a-t, *cat*)?	
Does the child have a degree of 'face blindness' (prosopagnosia)?	

Visual discrimination	
Does the child have difficulties discriminating between/sorting similar letters and digits (e.g. *a/o* or 2/5)?	
Does the child have difficulties discriminating between/sorting similar words (e.g. *was/saw*)?	
Does the child have difficulties discriminating between numerical and other symbols (e.g. x, ÷, + and −) and punctuation marks e.g. ;,)?	
Does the child reverse letters and digits, such as *b/d/p* or digits 2/5?	
Does the child 'see' the difference between letters such as *m* and *n*, or *n* and *u*?	
Does the child have difficulty finding a specific person in the class easily?	
Does the child have difficulties discriminating between symbols in core and non-core subjects?	
Does the child use upper-case letters inappropriately (e.g. in the middle of words)?	

Visual form constancy	
Does the child have difficulties reading words when the font, size or colour have changed?	
Does the child have difficulties recognising sums set out vertically instead of horizontally?	
Does the child recognise 2D shapes rotated or presented in different colours?	
Does the child have difficulties doing a jigsaw?	
Does the child have difficulties matching objects to pictures of that object?	
Does the child have difficulties recognising objects/people when small changes are made (e.g. a parent puts their hair up rather than having it down)?	
Does the child recognise objects seen from unfamiliar angles (e.g. wellie boots seen from the front/back)?	
Does the child understand that letters are the same despite different colours, fonts, sizes and so on?	
Does the child recognise a word if it is written in different orientations (i.e. vertically or horizontally)?	
Does the child reverse letters and digits?	
Does the child have difficulties reading and producing joined-up handwriting?	
Does the child have difficulties putting letters together to make words (e.g. c-a-t, *cat*?)	
Is the child having difficulty understanding that letters can be presented as either upper or lower case (e.g. *a* and *A*)?	

Visual figure ground	
Does the child have difficulty locating something on a busy whiteboard or in a busy display?	
Does the child have difficulties tidying up?	
Does the child have difficulty with word searches?	
Does the child have difficulties organising tools and equipment on their table?	

17

Does the child have difficulties finding details in illustrations?	
Does the child have difficulty finding specific words on a page?	
Is the child resistant to using dictionaries, a thesaurus, an encyclopaedia?	
Is the child unable to focus on the page but distracted by the illustrations?	
Does the child have difficulty looking at grid squares and graphing materials?	
Does the child have difficulties placing information in their books correctly?	
Does the child lose their place in a reading or writing text?	
Does the child confuse words and spaces between words in reading?	
Does the child have difficulties keeping their place when they are reading?	
Does the child have difficulties reading at speed?	
Does the child struggle to pick out information on a busy worksheet?	
Is the child easily confused by complicated diagrams, flowcharts and tables?	
Does the child have difficulty looking at complex patterns and colours?	
Does the child have difficulties colouring within spaces?	
Does the child have difficulties finding details in pictures and works of art?	
Does the child have difficulties finding equipment on a table top among other items?	

Visual motor integration	
Does the child have difficulty throwing and catching a ball and managing other PE apparatus (e.g. a tennis racket)?	
Does the child appear clumsy (e.g. knocks over pencil or paint pots easily)?	
Does the child have difficulty dressing?	
Does the child have difficulty writing?	
Does the child have difficulties knowing 'where' to start on a page?	
Does the child have difficulties organising their work on the page?	
Does the child have difficulties recalling letter and digit orientation?	
Does the child have difficulties orientating shoes to the correct feet?	
Does the child have difficulties with shape, space and pattern tasks?	
Does the child have difficulties drawing?	
Does the child have difficulties creating and/or copying 3D models?	

Creating a classroom that supports children with visual perception differences

A classroom organised to be supportive of learners with visual perception differences is a learner-friendly classroom, since all learners will benefit from strategies put in place to support those with visual perception differences.

When working with the child in each aspect of visual perception, there are some important considerations in terms of both Quality First Teaching strategy and observation. The following list is divided into sections containing suggestions for each Aspect. Different suggestions will be appropriate for different age groups and children. Some of the ideas will be appropriate for your situation, whereas there will be good reasons why others are less suitable for you. You should take from this list only what is relevant for the learners in your classroom and for you.

For children struggling with visual/spatial memory

- Point at what you are talking about.
- Give pictures to your words where possible and allow the child time to process the visual information.
- Allow the child to move into and through empty spaces rather than with large numbers of peers.
- Underline and mark positions on pages where the child is to begin and end pieces of writing.
- Provide card writing frames/spaces so the child knows where on the page to place text and illustrations.
- Mark the left margin with green pen and the right margin with red pen.
- Provide opportunities for pre-tutoring and post-tutoring of all material, but especially opportunities to talk about visual aspects of tasks.
- Provide opportunity to 'over-learn' information.
- Make class spaces obvious and easily accessible if possible. Leave as much space between objects as possible.
- Label spaces with visual symbols and/or photographs.
- Where appropriate, leave visual information accessible (e.g. on your whiteboard).

For children struggling with visual sequential memory

- Teach memory strategies specifically. Teach mnemonics to help remember items. Teach the child to create a memory narrative; that is, if the child has to recall three items (car, umbrella and bread), the child should create a narrative to aid recall. For example: '*I went out in my **car** because it was raining. I took an **umbrella** for when I got to the shop to buy the **bread**.*' Teach the child to verbally rehearse and maintain items in memory.

- Make observations regarding the items that are retrieved/not retrieved and where in the sequence the items are consistently retrieved fall. For example, if the child is retrieving items at the beginning of the sequence, this usually indicates that the child has a rehearsal strategy and is therefore maintaining the items in short-term memory. Additionally, the child may be recalling only items at the end of the sequence, which is usually indicative of the child recalling items that are temporally most recent.

- Teach the child to 'chunk' items for recall, that is, instead of remembering '1, 9, 6, 3' recall either '19, 63' or '1963'.

- Teach the child to recall items using a semantic link strategy. For example: dustpan/brush, knife/fork/spoon.

- If the child is struggling to recall a serial order of items, sit opposite the child. Ensure that your body midline is opposite theirs. When you place the items in front of the child arrange them in relation to their midline. For example, if there are three items to remember sequentially, place one on the left of the child's midline, one at the midline and one on the right of the midline. Point to their sides and their midline as you name their items. This may help to create a more stable visualisation of the items to be recalled. In this way, teaching of the alphabet or the number sequence 1 to 20 should be arranged in relation to the child's body midline. If you are then teaching numbers to 20, you could colour-code the numbers in four blocks: 0–5, 6–10, 11–15, 16–20. You may find that the child learns this more easily if they are taught to recall items in blocks as they relate to themselves.

- Use an alphabet arc when you teach the alphabet: it is easier to remember (for example) 'l m n o' as letters at the top of the arc than simply as part of a long line.

- Colour-code spellings – phonological vocabulary and sight vocabulary.

- Colour-code processes in Numeracy, such as HTU (hundreds tens units), in order that the child is able to recall which place holds which value.

- Write instructions down for the child on a task board, *but* ensure that the task board is not over-cluttered. Begin with a small number of steps and work up.

- Provide a symbol sequence for complex processes.

- When information is to be copied, place the text to be copied directly in front of the child. Do not automatically expect the child to record information from the class whiteboard to their book. Some children will need the text to be copied to be written in their book on the line above where they are copying.

- Work regularly on visual sequencing skills.

For children struggling with visual closure

- Ensure that all worksheets are clear and well presented.
- Discard worksheets that have not printed well.
- Ensure that the child's view of visual material is uninterrupted.
- Support word-building where necessary with concrete apparatus.
- Be mindful that extended reading can be very fatiguing and it may well be that the child is resistant to reading at length.

For children struggling with visual discrimination

- Use colour-coding to aid discrimination.
- Colour-code letters and digits.
- When teaching new information, particularly with letters/words and so on, try to avoid teaching visually similar items together (e.g. *b* and *d*, or *was* and *saw*).
- Experiment with coloured papers as bases for worksheets and display backgrounds to find the colours that best suit the child.
- Whenever possible, provide the child with concrete materials to manipulate, in order to augment visually processed information. Essentially, provide additional sensory input. When teaching letter sounds, give magnetic letters to feel and explore; or if it is appropriate to the child's developmental level, write words with a glue stick and cover them in sand so the child can both feel and see the word they are learning.

For children struggling with visual form constancy

- Use the same font when creating worksheets and class display labels. Be consistent in your use of font.
- Teach flexibility specifically, by playing games that encourage the child to make small changes to their activities. For example, they should be encouraged to add bricks to their model so that it looks different, though it is essentially the same model.
- Provide regular access to and opportunities for creative constructive and manipulative play.

For children struggling with visual figure ground

- De-clutter your classroom environment.
- Sit the child near you during whole-class activities.
- Avoid giving the child a seating position near passing classroom traffic.
- Provide an uninterrupted view of the teacher. Seat the child slightly to the side so they are able to take cues from peers if necessary. Alternatively, allow the child to sit on a chair if peers are seated on the carpeted floor.
- Avoid delivering teaching in front of busy displays or electronic equipment that is switched on.
- Organise and present displays clearly.

- Ensure that worksheets are differentiated to allow the child access. Simplify worksheets and enlarge them if necessary.
- Highlight important headings and chunks of text.
- De-clutter the child's immediate environment (table, desk).

For children struggling with visual motor integration

Important note: For children with visual motor integration difficulties/perceptual difficulties, you may consider marking or painting the edges of steps and stairs. Advice regarding adaptation of the environment should be sought from specialist outreach services.

- Develop gross motor skills to aid fine motor skills.
- Ensure that actions are performed with large movements to ensure that the child has the best chance to develop a sense of the movements required.
- Send the child into empty spaces before their peers. Avoid sending them to the carpet when all their peers are already seated (thus creating an obstacle course). Help the child avoid busy cloakrooms.
- Choose a seating arrangement close to the classroom door so the child does not have to navigate across the busy room.
- In PE, consider equipment that may travel more slowly; for example, airflow balls and balloons.
- Give the child their own whiteboard from which to copy, rather than the class whiteboard, or even write in their book and ask the child to copy directly beneath.
- Demarcate in exercise books where illustrations should be placed.
- Use sensory paper (i.e. paper with writing lines that are raised).
- Use paper with pegs to demarcate the positions of letters and spaces (spacing paper).
- Place a green spot to show where to begin writing and a red spot to show where to stop writing. Additionally, it may be helpful to the child to draw a green line down the left margin of the page and a red line down the right margin. This will help the child to return to the left margin each time and to stop at the right-hand side.
- Colour alternate line spaces on lined paper so the child can see where to place lettering.
- Embolden writing lines and consider over-colouring them red and green alternately.

How to use this book

You will find a simple five-step summary of how to use this book on page 26.

Every child with visual perception differences has different strengths and weaknesses. The priority for addressing these will be determined by the difficulties currently being faced by the child and will depend on your professional judgement, supported by the child's current anxieties.

To support you with focused target setting, the book is structured as follows:

- Seven different Aspects of visual perception have been identified (see Fig. 2 on page 24). Think about the child's difficulties: which of these Aspects is causing most concern at the moment?
- Within each Aspect there are four different Target Ladders, each based on a particular area of challenge. This is intended to help you to think carefully about precisely where the barrier may be.
- The relevant Target Ladder can then be used to identify the 'next step' target for the child.
- Suggested activities and strategies offer classroom-friendly ideas so you can support the child to meet their target.

For example, as you can see in Fig. 3 on page 25, difficulties with **Aspect 6: Visual figure ground** can be subdivided into specific areas to work on: Locating and isolating objects; Locating and isolating parts of pictures; Locating and isolating letters and words; and Saccade Control and depth perception. Each Target Ladder contains between 26 and 36 targets.

Aspects, Target Ladders and targets

Aspects

The seven different Aspects identified in this book describe contexts and difficulties which are frequently faced by children who have visual perception differences. In order to identify the most appropriate Aspect for a particular child, you will need to consider the most significant barrier for the child: for example, is it that the child is unable to isolate specific details in a busy visual image, or is the child struggling to recall high-frequency words/letter strings?

The Aspects of visual perception identified in this book are:

1 Visual memory skills
2 Visual sequential memory
3 Visual closure
4 Visual discrimination
5 Visual form constancy
6 Visual figure ground
7 Visual motor integration

Target Ladders

Each of the Aspects is further subdivided into four Target Ladders, each of which addresses different parts of the Aspect. These enable you to develop your understanding of the child's individual needs, 'drilling down' to assist you to identify the child's particular strengths and weaknesses. The Target Ladders are set out on pages 40–95.

SEN	7 Aspects	28 Target Ladders	Targets
VISUAL PERCEPTION	1 Visual memory skills	Attributes of and changes to a single object: size, colour, shape Attributes of and changes to a 2D image of an object Attributes of and changes to shapes and symbols Attributes of and changes to words, letters and digits	26 targets 26 targets 26 targets 26 targets
	2 Visual sequential memory	Recognising and continuing patterns Recognising and understanding serial order and associated vocabulary Recalling multiple items in serial order Recalling letter patterns	26 targets 26 targets 26 targets 26 targets
	3 Visual closure	Guessing an object from parts Dividing larger objects to find smaller parts Building larger objects from smaller parts Letters, syllables and words	26 targets 26 targets 26 targets 26 targets
	4 Visual discrimination	Identifying item attributes Recognising and identifying item changes Identifying, comparing and making the same (matching/ordering) Discriminating letters and sounds	26 targets 26 targets 26 targets 26 targets
	5 Visual form constancy	Recognising and identifying same/different in size, position and number Recognising and identifying same/different in rotation Recognising and identifying same/different in laterality Recognising and identifying same/different in vertical inversion	26 targets 26 targets 26 targets 26 targets
	6 Visual figure ground	Locating and isolating objects Locating and isolating parts of pictures Locating and isolating letters and words Saccade Control and depth perception	26 targets 26 targets 26 targets 26 targets
	7 Visual motor integration	Moving in space Hand–eye Drawing and colouring Writing	26 targets 36 targets 36 targets 35 targets

Fig. 2: The structure of *Target Ladders: Visual Perception*. Each Aspect has four Target Ladders.

Targets

There are up to 36 targets in each Target Ladder, with the simplest ones labelled with the letter A, then moving through the alphabet up to M (Q in Aspect 7), which are the most difficult. In each Target Ladder there are two (or more) rows that are labelled with the same letter, because all of the targets in those rows are at a similar developmental level. It is unlikely that any child will need to have all of the targets in each letter band: use your knowledge of the child to identify what they already know and to prioritise what is important.

Letter	Locating and isolating objects	Locating and isolating parts of pictures	Locating and isolating letters and words	Saccade Control and depth perception
E	Locates local objects while tracking horizontally left to right	Completes a grid search (2×2, 3×3 and so on) to locate items of a single attribute (e.g. colour)	Matches like letters, digraphs and trigraphs from a field of dissimilar distractors	Completes a simple straight-edged maze
E	Locates local objects while tracking vertically top to bottom	Completes a grid search (2×2, 3×3 and so on) to locate items of more than one attribute (e.g. specific shapes of given colour)	Matches like letters, digraphs and trigraphs from a field of similar distractors	Completes simple curved-edge maze
F	Locates local items in a random group of unrelated objects	Completes a grid search (2×2, 3×3 and so on) to locate an object	Completes an organised grid search (3×3, 4×4) to locate individual letters	Completes complex straight- and curved-edge mazes

Fig. 3: Part of the Target Ladders table for **Aspect 6: Visual figure ground** showing how targets are structured in the ladders.

Although within each Target Ladder rows with the same letter are similar, this is not the case between the different Target Ladders. So a child may have an A target in one ladder and a G target in another. Some of the Target Ladders start at a very early developmental level, whereas others assume a level of competence even in the A rows. Again, use your professional judgement and be guided by the child's abilities and needs. The letters are simply there to help you to identify targets which are at approximately the same developmental level within the same Target Ladder.

The targets are all written in positive language. This is to support you when you:

- look through them to find out what the child *can already* do;
- use them as the basis of the target you set for the child.

As you track the statements through each ladder, identifying what the child can already do, be aware of missed steps. If a child has missed one of the steps, further progress up that ladder may be insecure. Many children learn to mask the missed step, using developing skills in other areas to help them, but the time may come when the missed step will cause difficulties.

25

Activities and strategies to achieve the targets

In the Target Ladders on pages 40–95, targets are listed on left-hand pages. The corresponding right-hand pages offer ideas for activities or strategies that you might use to help to achieve the targets. These are suggestions only – but many have been used successfully in classrooms and are accepted good practice. Here, however, the activities or strategies are shown at the point in the developmental process at which they are likely to make the most impact.

The suggested activities can often be adapted to work for a range of targets within this stage of the ladder. For this reason, activities are generally not linked to individual targets.

How to set targets: A five-step summary

1. **Use Fig. 2 on page 24 to identify the one or two Aspects of visual perception differences that are most challenging for the child.** Please use the list of indicators on pages 15–18 for guidance.

2. **Turn to the Scope and Sequence Charts on pages 32–39.** These charts will help you pinpoint the specific targets you need – a more detailed explanation is given on page 32. The Scope and Sequence charts show the *upper limit* of the targets reached in each Target Ladder in each Aspect. Use these to gain an indication of where in the book you are likely to find appropriate targets.

3. **In the Target Ladders tables on pages 40–95, locate the targets** that you have identified from the Scope and Sequence charts and pinpoint specific ones for the child to work towards.

4. **Photocopy or print out from the CD the relevant targets page** so that you can:
   - highlight and date those the child can already do;
   - identify the next priorities.

5. **Use the Record of Progress sheet on page 29 to create a copy of the targets for the child or their parents.**

Making the most of Target Ladders

You may find the following tips helpful when setting your targets.

- Talk to the child about what they would like to improve.
- Discuss targets with the child's parents/carers.
- Think about your main concerns about that child's learning.

  A target that the child wants to improve is more likely to be successful.

- Once you have identified the Aspect, use the Scope and Sequence charts on pages 32–39 to identify the most beneficial Target Ladder and ascertain which page to start on.
  - Look for any 'missed steps', and target those first. The child is likely to find success fairly quickly and will be motivated to continue to try to reach new targets.
  - Talk to the child and agree an appropriate target based on your skills inventory. Again, targets which the child is aware of tend to be achieved most quickly and are motivational.
- The target does not have to be the lowest unachieved statement in any ladder: use your professional judgement and knowledge of the child to identify the most useful and important target for the child.
- No child will follow all of the targets in precisely the order listed. Use your professional judgement, and your knowledge about what the child can already do, to identify the most appropriate target and be realistic in your expectations. There may be some zigzagging up and down a column.
- When setting targets, always ask yourself practical questions:
  - What can I put in place in order to enable the child to meet the targets?
  - Which people and resources are available to support the child?
  - What is the likelihood of a child achieving a target within the next half-term?
  - Which targets have been agreed with other children in the class?

It is important that the targets you set are realistic considering the time, the adult support and the resources available.

Once you have identified what the child can already achieve, continue to highlight and update the sheets each time the child achieves a new target. Celebrate progress with the child while, at the same time, constantly checking to ensure that previously achieved targets remain secure. If any target becomes insecure, revisit it briefly, without setting a formal target, in order to give the child an opportunity to consolidate the skill without feeling that they are going backwards in their achievements.

Records of Progress

Creating a Record of Progress

If the child can communicate confidently, arrange to meet with them and their parents and ask them first to tell you what they are good at. When working with the child, you may need to adapt the immediate visual environment to support the child. For example, any task sheet may need to be simplified and/or enlarged. You may wish to colour-code the chart or consider carefully the colour of paper and text, or the style of font. Record their responses on the Record of Progress (RoP). A blank form is supplied for you to copy on page 29 and on the CD. Ask the child and their parents then to tell you which areas they would most like to improve.

If your school operates a Pupil Passport system, then you may want to amend the RoP form, but you will nonetheless need a sheet that can be annotated and amended.

As you add one or two more targets, talk to the child and their parents to check that they agree that each target is relevant and that they understand what they will need to do to achieve their targets. Targets that children do not know or care about are much harder for them to achieve. Limit the number of targets to a maximum of three. Remember, you do not need to use the precise wording of the targets given in this book: adapt the words to match the maturity and understanding of the learner. Monitor the impact of any intervention (see page 30) and review at regular intervals – at least half-termly – to see if there is an impact. If not, consider whether a different intervention would be more effective.

Principles for the effective use of an RoP include the following:

- The form must be 'live'. The child will need to have access to it at all times, as will all adults who work with the child, in order that it can be referred to, amended and updated regularly. Ensure that the child's parents/carers have a copy. If you think that the child is likely to lose or destroy their RoP, make a photocopy so that you can supply another.
- Together with the child, you have identified their priority areas to focus on. Management and support for these should be consistent across the school day and from all adults.
- As soon as each target has been achieved, according to the success criteria you agreed, the form should be dated and a 'next step' considered.
- When you set up the RoP, agree a review date which is ideally about half a term ahead and no more than one term ahead. Do not wait until this date to identify that targets have been achieved, but on this date review progress towards all targets – or identified next steps – and agree new targets.
- If a target has not been achieved, consider why not. If possible, try a different approach to meeting the target. Having the same target over and over is likely to bore the child and put them off following their RoP.

RECORD OF PROGRESS

Name _____ Class _____ Date agreed _____ Review date _____ RoP number: _____

My targets are	I will know that I have achieved my target when I can	Date when I achieved my target	Next steps
I am good at			
I would like to be better at			
It helps me when			

Targets approved by: Pupil _____ Teacher _____

SENCo _____ Parent/Carer _____

Monitoring a Record of Progress

In order to ensure that your Record of Progress (RoP) is used effectively, you need to monitor progress towards the targets each time you offer support. Use a monitoring sheet; a photocopiable example is given on page 31 and on the CD.

- Use a separate sheet – copied on to different coloured paper – for each target.
- Write the child's name at the top of the sheet and the target underneath.
- On each occasion when someone works with the child towards the target, they should write the smaller, more specific target that you are working towards *during this session* in the Target box.
- They should then write a comment. On each occasion the child achieves the target during the session and then back in class, tick the box.

The intention is that these sheets should be used to create a cumulative record of a child's progress towards their target. The evidence here can be used to assess the impact of an intervention in order that its appropriateness can be evaluated swiftly and any additional actions can be taken promptly.

What precisely you record will depend on the type of support being offered and the nature of the target.

- If you are delivering a planned intervention, make a record of the unit/page/activity and a comment about the learning the child demonstrated. For example, a comment relating to a target about the child's ability to remember a string of items may be: *'Told me the three correct items but did not recall the colours in serial order'*.
- If you are offering support in the classroom, you might want to comment on the child's learning over a few lessons. Focus on what the child has achieved in the lessons and whether the learning is secure.
- As a general principle, aim to include more positive than negative comments, and always try to balance a negative with a positive comment.

At the half-termly review of the RoP, collect together all of the monitoring sheets and look at the frequency of the comments against each target as well as the learning they reflect. If a child has had absences, or an intervention has not happened as often as planned, consider what impact that has had on the effectiveness of the intervention. If the intervention has gone as planned, look at the progress charted and ask yourself these questions:

- Is it swift enough? Is the intervention helping this child to close the gap? Is the adult working with the child the best person for the job?
- Is this the best intervention? Is there anything else you can reasonably do in school?
- What should happen next? If the intervention was successful, do you continue it, develop it, consolidate it or change to a different target?

At the end of the process, create a new RoP with the child and their parents/carers and use a new monitoring sheet.

Monitoring the progress of _____ towards meeting the

target of _____

Date	Target	Comment	Achieved			

Scope and Sequence charts

The Scope and Sequence charts can be used to help you to pinpoint targets, following the advice on pages 26–27. Once you have identified the Aspect(s) you wish to focus on:

1. Find the relevant page in the Scope and Sequence charts on pages 33–39. Look for the Aspect name here:

2. Identify the Target Ladders that match the skills you wish to target. Look for the names of the ladders here:

3. Read down the list of targets here: The targets shown here are from the highest level for the ladder on that page. If the first target listed is too easy, look at the next target beneath it. Continue down the list until you reach a target that is beyond the child's current attainment.

4. Find the page number, shown here: Turn to that page and read all the targets on it. One of them should be appropriate. If not, turn to the previous or subsequent page.

Scope and Sequence Aspect 6: Visual figure ground

Locating and isolating objects

Page	Letters	Target Ladder focus	Focus of suggested activities
80	A–D	Directs gaze at a specific item when dissimilar items are at a variety of heights	What am I looking at?
82	E–G	Locates local specific item in a disorganised table top array	Hide and Seek
84	H–J	Locates items, from a complex background	Object hunt
86	K–M	Retrieves item when given verbal instruction	Treasure hunt

Locating and isolating parts of pictures

Page	Letters	Target Ladder focus	Focus of suggested activities
80	A–D	Locates which quarter of the image the adult is looking at	What are you looking at?
82	E–G	Completes a grid search up to 4×4 in an image creating a busy background for a single item	Grid search
84	H–J	Identifies object in three-quarters of picture	Picture fractions
86	K–M	Colours three objects that appear as *top* or *middle* or *bottom* in an illustration	Tracing objects

Fig. 4: Part of the Scope and Sequence chart for **Aspect 6: Visual figure ground**.

Bear in mind the following:

- If the wording of the target is not precisely accurate for your child, modify it to make it appropriate.
- Different children may meet the target statements in a slightly different order. The order shown is approximate and true for many children. Adapt the order in which you set the targets for the individual child.
- No child is expected to be given all of the targets on the page. A range of small steps targets is shown in order to give you the widest possible variety of targets from which to select.
- If you cannot find a target which meets your needs, use the other targets to give you an idea of the level expected, and write your own target. It is important that all of the targets on the Record of Progress are appropriate for the individual child.

Scope and Sequence Aspect 1: Visual memory skills

Attributes of and changes to a single object

Page	Letters	Target Ladder focus	Focus of suggested activities
40	A–D	Responds to questions about a range of object attributes	Guess what?
42	E–G	When asked, can name a number of objects shown from unrelated categories	Guess which?
44	H–J	Remembers more than one object removed simultaneously from a group	Guess how?
46	K–M	Remembers and recreates a simple design in 3D using up to ten blocks	Guess where?

Attributes of and changes to a 2D image of an object

Page	Letters	Target Ladder focus	Focus of suggested activities
40	A–D	Remembers whether an item was to the left or right/above or below a given item in a photograph	What can you see?
42	E–G	Remembers the odd item out in simple patterns	Odd one out
44	H–J	Identifies pictures missing from a group	What's changed?
46	K–M	Matches six randomly positioned pairs from memory	Picture matching

Attributes of and changes to shapes and symbols

Page	Letters	Target Ladder focus	Focus of suggested activities
40	A–D	Matches an identical shape with three variables changed	Match it up
42	E–G	Finds a shape sequence in a given pattern	Sort them out
44	H–J	Remembers whether a symbol is pointing up or down	Symbols
46	K–M	Recreates from memory a simple line-drawn symbol/picture with up to six parts	Who's where?

Attributes of and changes to words, letters and digits

Page	Letters	Target Ladder focus	Focus of suggested activities
40	A–D	When shown a digit/single letter, is able to find it within a group of flash cards	Letters and logos
42	E–G	Compares like digit strings to identify digit changes	Remembering letters and digits
44	H–J	Matches pairs of target CVC words among distractors	What's what?
46	K–M	Recalls colour of specific digraphs/trigraphs, digits or words and finds them in a simple sentence	What's where?

33

Scope and Sequence Aspect 2: Visual sequential memory

Recognising and continuing patterns

Page	Letters	Target Ladder focus	Focus of suggested activities
48	A–D	In a sequence of first and last, can predict the medial *next* event	Picture sequencing
50	E–G	Organises items into a two-step repeating pattern independently	Copying simple sequences
52	H–J	Continues and explains simple five-step repeating patterns with apparatus	Recognising complex patterns
54	K–M	Draws own complex repeating pattern	Building and drawing patterns

Recognising and understanding serial order and associated vocabulary

Page	Letters	Target Ladder focus	Focus of suggested activities
48	A–D	Names items/person in medial position	Who comes where?
50	E–G	Uses ordinal language to denote position up to tenth place	Order, order!!
52	H–J	Creates a sequence with a number of items between three and ten	First, next, last
54	K–M	Recalls up to five items and their position in a five-step sequence	Recalling position

Recalling multiple items in serial order

Page	Letters	Target Ladder focus	Focus of suggested activities
48	A–D	Recalls five items with single attribute of colour, in serial order	Colour sequencing
50	E–G	Recalls five items with a change to a single attribute of left/right orientation	Remembering one thing
52	H–J	Recalls up to five items in serial order with three attributes of shape, size and colour	Remembering everything
54	K–M	Recalls up to five similar plain line-drawn symbols with changes to size and orientation	Symbol eyes

Recalling letter patterns

Page	Letters	Target Ladder focus	Focus of suggested activities
48	A–D	Copies a trigraph or more than one digraph in one viewing	Letter patterns
50	E–G	Recalls a single-syllable word with a digraph/trigraph preceding the vowel	Remembering words
52	H–J	Recalls two related words accurately	Pretty poly
54	K–M	Copies complex sentence from model in further distance (class whiteboard)	Total recall

34

Scope and Sequence Aspect 3: Visual closure

Guessing an object from parts

Page	Letters	Target Ladder focus	Focus of suggested activities
56	A–D	Recognises a picture as pieces are provided one at a time	Bits and pieces
58	E–G	Identifies picture theme from two image parts	Picture perfect
60	H–J	Closes simple line-drawn shape with one side omitted	One at a time
62	K–M	Guesses image hidden in a simple colour-by-numbers	Dot-to-dots

Dividing larger objects to find smaller parts

Page	Letters	Target Ladder focus	Focus of suggested activities
56	A–D	Cuts up a picture and matches parts to original image	Taking it apart
58	E–G	Finds specific piece in 12-piece puzzle from an image	Matching parts
60	H–J	Predicts resulting parts when a picture of an object cut into quarters	What was that?
62	K–M	Finds a word in a word search grid	What's wrong?

Building larger objects from smaller parts

Page	Letters	Target Ladder focus	Focus of suggested activities
56	A–D	Copies connected brick pattern using six bricks	Building block patterns
58	E–G	Can complete a simple picture cut in half horizontally	Matching halves
60	H–J	Completes three-quarters of a puzzle	Puzzles and pieces
62	K–M	Uses bricks to build a model with multiple stages and parts	Brick building

Letters, syllables and words

Page	Letters	Target Ladder focus	Focus of suggested activities
56	A–D	Recognises CVC words from dotted and dashed outlines	Seeing small words
58	E–G	Identifies missing letter combinations from their dashed outlines	Guess the word
60	H–J	Suggests letters/phonemes missing from outline of words	What's missing?
62	K–M	Predicts missing words in a paragraph	Words and sentences

Scope and Sequence Aspect 4: Visual discrimination

Identifying item attributes			
Page	**Letters**	**Target Ladder focus**	**Focus of suggested activities**
64	A–D	Is able to identify basic concepts of pattern	Basic concepts
66	E–G	Finds items with common features	Have or have not?
68	H–J	Finds an item of a given orientation in an image	Picture treasure hunt
70	K–M	Finds a number of objects with a given attribute	Picture perfect treasure hunt

Recognising and identifying item changes			
Page	**Letters**	**Target Ladder focus**	**Focus of suggested activities**
64	A–D	Compares multiple items to identify multiple differences	Spot the difference
66	E–G	Recognises a change to physical appearance of a less familial person	Changeabout
68	H–J	Recognises a combination of attribute changes	All change
70	K–M	Identifies multiple objects removed from a group	More or less?

Identifying, comparing and making the same (matching/ordering)			
Page	**Letters**	**Target Ladder focus**	**Focus of suggested activities**
64	A–D	Matches items on the basis of colour	Matching items
66	E–G	Matches items on the basis of quantity	Similarities
68	H–J	Sorts items with a combination of attributes	Sort it out
70	K–M	Recognises the same object in different orientations against different visually complex backgrounds	All sorted

Discriminating letters and sounds			
Page	**Letters**	**Target Ladder focus**	**Focus of suggested activities**
64	A–D	Matches lower-case letters which are hanging: *g, p, j. q, y*	Lower-case lookout
66	E–G	Identifies which letters have curved edges on left or right-hand edge/top or bottom	Letter shapes
68	H–J	Identifies letters which are hanging from a mixture of short/tall/hanging	Type-writer
70	K–M	Sorts words into pairs with slightly different strings of letters	Odd words

Scope and Sequence Aspect 5: Visual form constancy

Recognising and identifying same/different size, position and number			
Page	Letters	Target Ladder focus	Focus of suggested activities
72	A–D	Sorts and discriminates large/medium/ small/identical items	Big or small?
74	E–G	Identifies odd one out according to size, position or number	Matching position and number
76	H–J	Sorts identical shapes in order of size, small to large	Size it up
78	K–M	Finds the same words of different sizes and different fonts	Word hunt

Recognising and identifying same/different in rotation			
Page	Letters	Target Ladder focus	Focus of suggested activities
72	A–D	Recognises which object has been rotated	Turning around
74	E–G	Rotates objects through one whole turn on request	How far to turn?
76	H–J	Finds simple curved-edged shape that matches model	Rotation
78	K–M	Sorts d/p and 6/9	Rotation continues

Recognising and identifying same/different in laterality			
Page	Letters	Target Ladder focus	Focus of suggested activities
72	A–D	Identifies aspects of a single object that fall within a left laterality	Which way round?
74	E–G	Corrects laterality of odd one out	Matches laterality
76	H–J	Can laterally invert a complex shape	Odd directions
78	K–M	Recognises d in b distractors	Orientating letters horizontally

Recognising and identifying same/different in vertical inversion			
Page	Letters	Target Ladder focus	Focus of suggested activities
72	A–D	Given two objects, can say which one is incorrectly vertically organised	Up or down?
74	E–G	Corrects orientation of odd one out	Upside down all sorted
76	H–J	Can vertically invert a complex shape	Odd way up
78	K–M	Recognises d in p distractors	Orientating letters vertically

Scope and Sequence Aspect 6: Visual figure ground

Locating and isolating objects

Page	Letters	Target Ladder focus	Focus of suggested activities
80	A–D	Directs gaze at a specific item when dissimilar items are at a variety of heights	What am I looking at?
82	E–G	Locates local specific item in a disorganised table top array	Hide and Seek
84	H–J	Locates items, from a complex background	Object hunt
86	K–M	Retrieves item when given verbal instruction	Treasure hunt

Locating and isolating parts of pictures

Page	Letters	Target Ladder focus	Focus of suggested activities
80	A–D	Locates which quarter of the image the adult is looking at	What are you looking at?
82	E–G	Completes a grid search up to 4×4 in an image creating a busy background for a single item	Grid search
84	H–J	Identifies object in three-quarters of picture	Picture fractions
86	K–M	Colours three objects that appear as *top* or *middle* or *bottom* in an illustration	Tracing objects

Locating and isolating letters and words

Page	Letters	Target Ladder focus	Focus of suggested activities
80	A–D	Locates letter strings in a disorganised visual field of ten distractors	Hunt the letter
82	E–G	Completes an organised grid search (5×5, 6×6 and so on) to locate words with similar letter distractors	Word searching
84	H–J	Locates letters, digraphs and trigraphs on a page	Letters on a page
86	K–M	Locates the same word on a page	Words on a page

Saccade Control and depth perception

Page	Letters	Target Ladder focus	Focus of suggested activities
80	A–D	Tracks with eyes to follow a path with a combination of top to bottom and left to right on horizontal surface	Top, middle or bottom?
82	E–G	Tracks ahead in a complex maze to plan route	Mazes
84	H–J	Demonstrates Saccade Control to track sentences across a paragraph where text runs onto lines below	Saccade Control
86	K–M	Organises objects into *top/middle/bottom* position	Foreground–background

Scope and Sequence Aspect 7: Visual motor integration

Moving in space

Page	Letters	Target Ladder focus	Focus of suggested activities
88	A–D	Maintains appropriate distance from others	Turning head to look
90	E–H	Successfully changes direction to avoid a corner, safely turning right	Avoiding obstacles
92	I–L	Moves purposefully in a range of directions and changes direction	Avoiding moving obstacles
94	M	Can co-ordinate movement with others for a specific purpose	Team games

Hand-eye

Page	Letters	Target Ladder focus	Focus of suggested activities
88	A–D	Transitions gaze around aspects of objects being manipulated	Looking and pointing
90	E–H	Throws balls to another person	Tracking and retrieving
92	I–L	Catches balls of a range of sizes	Throwing and catching
94	M–Q	Cuts around simple geometric shapes	Finger play

Drawing and colouring

Page	Letters	Target Ladder focus	Focus of suggested activities
88	A–D	Stops random scribble in defined spaces	Scribbling
90	E–H	Makes marks that cross the body midline diagonally	Controlling tools
92	I–L	Draws accurately between a range of points	Colouring and drawing
94	M–P	Draws a recognisable picture independently from memory	Drawing and colouring confidently

Writing

Page	Letters	Target Ladder focus	Focus of suggested activities
88	A–D	Makes multiple random marks	Making patterns
90	E–H	Copies vertical marks	Starting and stopping to draw accurately between points
92	I–L	Draws and closes curved line shapes (circle, oval)	Tracing lines, symbols and letters
94	M–Q	Writes sitting on lines	Learning to reproduce letter shapes and patterns

The Target Ladders

Letter	Attributes of and changes to a single object: size, colour, shape	Attributes of and changes to a 2D image of an object	Attributes of and changes to shapes and symbols	Attributes of and changes to words, letters and digits
A	Identifies an object shown previously	Identifies an item from a photograph	Identifies correctly whether an item has/has not been seen before	Remembers shop names from signs/logos
A	Identifies a familiar object from a group of unfamiliar objects	Locates a given item in a photograph	Finds a shape that is different to one shown	Matches logo to logo
B	Remembers the colour of an object	Remembers at least one item from a photograph	Finds an identical shape from a selection of shapes	Recalls items of printed text in the environment (e.g. labels, brand names)
B	Remembers up to three colours of an object	Responds to questions about the number of items in a photograph (e.g. 'How many trees?')	Matches an identically sized shape from a group	Remembers which number is shown (e.g. which number was on the door)
C	Remembers whether an object was large or small	Responds correctly to questions about the colour of a single item (e.g. 'What colour was the cat's tail?')	Matches an identical coloured shape from a group	Remembers which magnetic letter/digit was drawn from a bag
C	Remembers whether an object has curved and/or straight edges	Remembers which items were the same colour in a photograph	Matches pairs of shapes (no more than three)	Matches a letter/digit seen, given a choice of two magnetic letters
D	Responds to questions about more than one aspect of a single item (e.g. 'What colour was the coat?' and 'How many pockets did it have?')	Remembers which direction an object is facing (left or right laterality) (e.g. 'Was the car travelling to the left or the right?')	Matches an identical shape with two variables changed (e.g. size, colour)	Matches a letter/digit seen, given a choice of two letter flashcards
D	Responds to questions about a range of object attributes (e.g. 'What shape were the pockets?' and 'What colour was the zip?')	Remembers whether an item was to the left or right/above or below a given item in the photograph	Matches an identical shape with three variables changed (e.g. size, colour and shape)	When shown a digit/single letter, is able to find it within a group of flash cards

40

Suggested activities or strategies

Guess what?

Teach the child to recall the names of single items and to focus on recall of details about single items.

- Play Peek-a-boo. Using an object under a cloth or behind a screen, allow the child to look at the object briefly before removing it from view. Gradually decrease the amount of time the child is given to view the object before it is removed. Begin by asking the child to recall items from the same category. Support the child by teaching them to look for specific information about the object, such as colour, shape, size, use, function and so on.

What can you see?

Teach the child to remember items seen in a simple picture.

- Provide the child with a simple picture such as a photograph from home of a birthday party. Allow the child to look at the picture until they feel they are ready and then cover the picture. The child must remember some items from the picture. Keep a list of items in the picture and the child can score a point/ gain a token for each item recalled. This task can be differentiated by increasing or decreasing the amount of time the image is shown or by increasing/decreasing the number of items depicted.
- Use published books which are intended to teach young children vocabulary. Give the child time to look at a very simple picture for a designated amount of time. The child must then answer a question about the picture.

Match it up

Teach the child to match a range of shapes with a variety of attributes.

- Organise two groups of plane shapes in which each shape has a different colour and different size (attribute shapes). Give the child one set and spread them across the table. Place the other set in a feely bag. Ask the child to retrieve a shape from the bag, look at it, replace it and then find the identical shape from their set. Differentiate this task by encouraging the child to wait for a longer period before finding their shape.
- Play Shape Bingo. Make a Bingo card with a set of six different shapes, varying in size and colour. Draw a shape at a time from a bag and the child must hold this in memory while they look at their card.

Letters and logos

Teach the child to recall simple letter shapes.

- Agree with the child a small number of words. Write the words on card and stick them up around the school. Take the child on a letter/ number walk and encourage the child to recall where the items were seen.
- Photograph, name, match and sort either a range of common easily recognisable shop names, such as Asda or Sainsbury's, or a range of common logos, such as the McDonald's logo. There are published games and iPad apps that also support this skill.
- Provide opportunities to explore magnetic letters in order to match like letters of the same colour:
  ○ match like letters of the same colour;
  ○ match like letters that are different colours;
  ○ match photographs of a letter to a corresponding magnetic letter;
  ○ match letters to printed or hand-drawn letters;
  ○ match letters to simple written words.

41

Aspect 1: Visual memory skills

Letter	Attributes of and changes to a single object: size, colour, shape	Attributes of and changes to a 2D image of an object	Attributes of and changes to shapes and symbols	Attributes of and changes to words, letters and digits
E	Remembers a pair of related objects from a selection (e.g. dustpan and brush)	Remembers where the item was in relation to other features in the photograph (e.g. the man was in the bath)	Sorts similar shapes	Copies a simple string using correct letters/digits provided (three letters/digits)
E	Remembers a pair of unrelated objects from a selection (e.g. toothbrush and shoe)	Responds to questions and identifies relevant items contained in a simple photograph	Sorts shape from a given picture model (e.g. finds all the triangles that look like a given picture of a triangle)	Copies a simple string using correct letters when given distractors
F	Recalls objects from a mixed group that belong to a given category from a selection (e.g. remembers fruit in a box of toys)	Remembers related details from a picture to answer a question	Sorts shapes into groups according to one attribute (e.g. colour)	Copies a simple letter/digit string using a choice of six letters/digits provided
F	When asked, can name a number of objects shown from a specific category (e.g. can recall items of clothing)	Identifies what is 'wrong' in a picture	Sorts shapes into groups according to multiple attributes (e.g. colour, shape and size)	Copies a simple string of up to six letters using correct letters and di-/trigraphs when given distractors
G	Recalls an object that is unrelated to category	Remembers detail in simple patterns	Finds a shape in a given pattern	Compares two similar letter strings to identify letter changes
G	When asked, can name a number of objects shown from unrelated categories (e.g. apple, sunglasses, pen, chair)	Remembers the odd item out in simple patterns	Finds a shape sequence in a given pattern	Compares like digit strings to identify digit changes

Suggested activities or strategies

Guess which?

Teach the child to recall a range of items that are related or unrelated to given categories.

- Provide the child with a range of objects from a specific category (e.g. spoon, fork, knife, plate, napkin). The child should be given a time limit to look at these items and then recall as many as possible. This can be extended by mixing category items or including items that are semantically related (e.g. dustpan/brush).

Odd one out

Teach the child to recall relevant items in an image. Develop this skill to identifying items that are related or non-relevant.

- Teach the child the concept of 'important'. Discuss with the child the different aspects or items present in the image (e.g. bath time: shampoo/shower/towel = relevant, but vase/flowers/cup = non-relevant).
- Teach the child to recall items that may be related, such as: ambulance/man on stretcher/bike/tree. How many of these can the child recall?

Sort them out

Teach the child to recall a variety of shapes and shape attributes. This section can generally be differentiated for children by considering the orientation of shapes and using a variety of regular or irregular shapes. Consider also using invented shapes.

- Provide opportunities for the child to complete shape sorters/post shapes through holes.
- Provide the child with 2D plastic shapes and a sheet of outlines. Show the shape to the child before hiding it behind a screen. The child should then identify the outline of the shape shown on a page of outline choices. Differentiate the task by increasing or decreasing the number of outlines on the target choice page or by using one shape and showing the shape in a specific orientation which the child must choose from the target sheet.
- Provide opportunities to explore printing with objects/2D shapes and the sides of 3D shapes.
- Build simple shape pictures and patterns with plane shapes of different sizes and colours.

Remembering letters and digits

Teach the child to recall letter and digit strings correctly but also to identify any changes to the group.

- Use a Look, Cover, Recall, Write approach. The child should look at the letter/digit string until they feel they know it (or for a given time scale); it is then covered while they recall and reproduce the target string.
- Play Letter/Digit Dice. Provide the child with six dice that contain a range of different letters/digits. Encourage the child to roll the dice and to look at the letters that fall face up before they are removed from view. Begin by asking the child to remember as many of the letters/digits as possible and each time the child remembers an item correctly place the dice back in view.
- Play Digit String and Letter String Snap. Prepare two sets of cards with matching pairs of letter and/or digit strings. Play Snap in the traditional manner by dealing the cards equally to two players. Players turn their top cards over simultaneously and shout 'Snap!' when they match. The winner is the player with the most cards.
- Play Spot the Difference beween words. For example: *man, men*.

43

Aspect 1: Visual memory skills

Letter	Attributes of and changes to a single object: size, colour, shape	Attributes of and changes to a 2D image of an object	Attributes of and changes to shapes and symbols	Attributes of and changes to words, letters and digits
H	Recalls changes to object (e.g. remembers that the stick was large but now it is small)	Remembers and selects an image from series of images (e.g. can look at a Lotto board and find a card to match one of the pictures)	Recalls a symbol from a choice of two	When shown a simple CVC word, is able to remember the order of letters and rearrange letters given to re-create the word
H	Recalls changes to object parts (e.g. remembers that the teddy had a red bow but now it is blue)	Matches a series of images accurately (e.g. is able to complete a Lotto board independently)	Recalls up to three symbols	When shown a simple CVC word is able to collect and arrange letters independently
I	Remembers which object has been missing from a group	Identifies which piece does not belong to the Lotto group	Recalls name and detail of symbols missing from a group	Finds given target word in a pair of target word and distractor
I	Remembers which object has been added to a group	Identifies the 'odd one out' in a series of near-identical pictures	Recalls name and detail of symbols added to a group	Finds CVC words in a group of six given a target model (e.g. finds three *pan* words in a mixed set of *pan* and *man*)
J	Remembers more than one object added to a group simultaneously	Identifies pictures added to a group (e.g. which pieces do not belong to a puzzle)	Remembers whether a symbol is facing to the left or the right	Matches pairs of target CVC words
J	Remembers more than one object removed simultaneously from a group	Identifies pictures missing from a group (e.g. which pieces are missing from a simple puzzle)	Remembers whether a symbol is pointing up or down	Matches pairs of target CVC words among distractors

Suggested activities or strategies

Guess how?

Teach the child to recall a range of items that may be added to or removed from a group.

- Play Kim's Game. Objects are placed on a tray. The child is given time to look at the tray of objects before the tray is covered. The child must then remember as many items as possible from the tray. Give the child time to look at the objects before asking the child to look away while one item is removed or one item is added. The child must guess which item has been added or removed. This game can be extended by asking the child to remember more than one item added or removed and also by simultaneously adding *and* removing one or more items.
- Play a simple spot the change game. Place an object in front of the child. Ask the child to hide their eyes while you make a simple change (e.g. change the colour of the bow in the doll's hair). The child must spot the change.

What's changed?

Teach the child to recall and match pictures presented in an organised array.

- Play Lotto. Teach the child to match their pictures independently to their Lotto board. Give the Lotto board to the child and keep the cards yourself. Allow the child one card at a time to place onto the board. Extend this activity by placing one card among the group that does not belong to the group. Can the child identify which card is the odd one out at the beginning, having seen the board? If the child is not able to identify the odd one out, periodically allow the child to look at the full set of cards.

Symbols

Teach the child to recall simple symbols. These should not be recognisable as pictures or as letters but rather as computer 'call outs'. For example:

- Help the child to invent a name for each symbol that helps them associate meaning with the visual symbol. For example, for these symbols you might have: cross, doughnut, arrow, sand-timer, stairs.
- Play Misfits. Print each symbol onto card and cut it into thirds horizontally. Jumble up the pieces and encourage the child to put them back together. Remove the pieces that make one of the symbol characters. Can the child remember the names for the symbols they have created and remember what has been removed or added?
- Play Symbol Treasure Hunt. Place symbols (safely!) around the classroom. The child should look at a symbol then return to orientate an identical symbol correctly. Gradually increase the number of symbols to hold in memory.

What's what?

Teach the child to recall words and letter/digit strings. These should be both words and non-words.

- Create an empty grid and a set of letters, digits or words that can be placed in the grid. Arrange the letters, symbols or digits in the grid and allow the child time to view the configuration before asking the child to turn away. Remove an item from the grid. The child should be encouraged to remember which item was in the empty grid square or has been exchanged for another item. This task can be differentiated by showing the child a grid configuration of the items and encouraging them to use their items to make the same configuration from memory.
- Create a Colour-by-Letters/Digits words sheet. Colour each of the words in the key a different colour. Encourage the child to remember the colour of each word as they colour.
- Create a set of matching CVC word and non-word cards for the child to sort and organise.

Aspect 1: Visual memory skills

Letter	Attributes of and changes to a single object: size, colour, shape	Attributes of and changes to 2D image of object	Attributes of and changes to shapes and symbols	Attributes of and changes to words, letters and digits
K	Identifies non-sequential position of given objects in a group	Matches pairs seen briefly – says whether the pairs are same or different	Identifies non-sequential position of symbols in a 2×2 grid	Can match coloured digraphs/trigraphs
K	Identifies changes to the position of objects in a group	Matches pictures placed one pair at a time (e.g. Snap)	Identifies non-sequential position of symbols added to or removed from a 2×2 grid	Highlights given digraph/trigraph or digit in word or string
L	Remembers and re-creates a simple design in 2D using up to four simple shapes	Matches three pairs placed in an organised array from memory	Recreates from memory a simple grid of up to four symbols (2×2 grid)	Identifies word/letter/digits added to group (e.g. *jump/jump**ed***)
L	Remembers and re-creates a simple design in 2D using up to six simple shapes	Matches six pairs placed in an organised array from memory	Recreates from memory a simple grid of up to six symbols (2×3 grid)	Identifies word/letter/digits removed from group (e.g. *jump**er**/jump*)
M	Remembers and re-creates a simple design in 3D using up to six blocks	Matches three randomly positioned pairs from memory	Recreates from memory a simple line-drawn symbol/picture with up to three parts	Combines colour-coded letters and digraph/trigraphs to create modelled words
M	Remembers and re-creates a simple design in 3D using up to ten blocks	Matches six randomly positioned pairs from memory	Recreates from memory a simple line-drawn symbol/picture with up to six parts	Recalls colour of specific digraphs/trigraphs, digits or words and finds them in a simple sentence

Suggested activities or strategies

Guess where?

Teach the child to recall information about the position of single and multiple items.

- Play Lotto hide and seek. Children are shown a Lotto board. The pictures on the board are then covered one at a time. When all the pictures are covered the child must remember the position of specified pictures (e.g. *'Where was the cat?'*). This task can be simplified or made more difficult by decreasing or increasing the Lotto board size.
- Who's changed? Encourage the children to sit in a circle. The target child must try to memorise who is in the group and where they are sitting and then turn their back or leave the group. The adult should then choose two children to change places. The target child must then return to the group and guess which two children have changed places. Extend this activity by increasing the number of children who move and by making changes to the appearance of children (e.g. they take off glasses/shoes or turn jumpers around).
- Use a variety of lollipop sticks and matchsticks to create simple 2D designs for the child to copy and recall. To differentiate this task move onto block designs with bricks. The complexity of this task increases with the number of lollipop sticks or bricks.

Picture matching

Teach the child to recall and match pictures presented in a random presentation.

- Play Snap. Each player is dealt an equal number of picture cards or numbered suit playing cards. Simultaneously, the children place a card. If the cards match, the players shout *'Snap'*. The first person to shout *'Snap'* wins the cards on the table. If the cards do not match, then the players continue to place cards until they do match. The winning player is the player who has all or most of the playing cards.
- Play Pelmanism/Pairs. Play this game by turning pairs of cards over face down on the table. Shuffle the cards around. The players each take a turn to turn over two cards. If the cards match, the player may keep that pair of cards. If the cards do not match, play then passes to the other player. The winning player matches the greatest number of pairs.

What's where?

Teach the child to recall symbols and their non-sequential position.

- Create an empty grid and a set of symbols that can be placed in the grid. Arrange the symbols in the grid and allow the child time to view the configuration before asking the child to turn away. Remove a symbol from the grid. The child should be encouraged to remember which symbol was in the empty grid square or has been exchanged for another symbol.
- Place symbols in a grid. Provide the child with a set of identical pre-cut symbols and a grid of the same size. The child should be given an appropriate time to view the grid before it is removed. The child should then paste the symbols into their recalled positions on their own grid.
- Provide regular practice in tracing and copying symbols.

Remembering letter changes

Teach the child to identify digraphs/trigraphs.

- Word jigsaws. Provide the child with a range of simple words and non-words which have been coloured and cut up to show letters and digraphs/trigraphs. Allow the child a given time to look at a specific word on a flashcard. The child should then recall and reconstruct the word from memory using the letters and digraphs/trigraphs.
- Ask children to highlight digraphs/trigraphs with different colours in a sentence, for example, highlighting all the occurences of *igh* in the sentence: *They saw a bright light high in the sky before the fight.*

Aspect 2: Visual sequential memory

Letter	Recognising and continuing patterns	Recognising and understanding serial order and associated vocabulary	Recalling multiple items in serial order	Recalling letter patterns
A	Recalls relevant visual features that allow pictures to be sequenced	Understands and responds to associated vocabulary: *more*, *again*	Can name important attributes to look for when trying to recall	Distinguishes between pictures and letters
A	Uses relevant detail to sequence two related pictures	Understands additional sequential vocabulary: *before*, *after* and *then*	Recalls colour of first item on request	Distinguishes between letters and words
B	Orders two pictures on the basis of *now* and *next*	Understands language of sequence: *first*, *next*, *last*, *now*	Recalls colour of last item on request	Finds matching letter
B	Orders three pictures using *first*, *next*, *last*	Talks about a simple sequence using sequential vocabulary	Recalls any attribute of first or last item (e.g. colour)	Copies a two-letter word/non-word pattern
C	Predicts event post- and pre-sequence	Names items/person in first position	Recalls two items with single attribute of colour, in serial order	Copies a three-letter word/non-word pattern
C	In a sequence of *first* and *last*, can predict the medial *next* event	Names items/person in last position	Recalls three items with single attribute of colour, in serial order	Copies up to six-letter word/non-word pattern
D	Orders four related pictures and creates a simple related narrative	Names items/people in all positions: *first*, *next*, *last*	Recalls four items with single attribute of colour, in serial order	Copies single digraph in one viewing
D	Orders six related pictures and creates a simple related narrative	Names items/person in medial position	Recalls five items with single attribute of colour, in serial order	Copies a trigraph or more than one digraph in one viewing

Suggested activities or strategies

Picture sequencing

Teach the child to organise a set of pictures into a pictorial story that makes sense.

- Create simple pictorial diaries of the child's day. Talk about *before/after* breakfast or lunch. Ask them what was the last thing they did before coming to school/before playtime?
- Sequence pictures. Encourage the child to organise a set of pictures that depicts a simple sequence into an order that makes sense. Begin with two pictures depicting *first/last* (*now/next*) and work up to a sequence of four pictures. There are many published sets of sequencing cards that would be appropriate for this task; however, be mindful that a sequence depicting a social scenario requires more processing than a simple functional sequence such as a banana being peeled. Use sequence pictures that contain less visual information where possible.
- Introduce a visual timetable, showing activities to be done in school during each day. Review the sequence at the end of the day using the key vocabulary.

Who comes where?

Teach the child to understand and use the early language of sequence in relation to themselves.

- Play simple rule-based games such as Snakes and Ladders to see who comes *first*, *second*, *third*.
- Play hopscotch.
- Make a set of simple numbered stepping stones chalked on the ground. Roll a dice and encourage the child to walk on the given number of places.
- Discuss the children's positions when lining up for various activities.

Colour sequencing

Teach the child to recall a series of items in serial order with the single attribute of colour.

- Place a series of coloured chalk rings on the floor. Each ring should be a different colour. Make a corresponding set of colour flash cards. Create a sequence of coloured flash cards that the child must remember and then use to help them stand in each ring according to the colour sequence.
- Use paint colour charts. Teach the child to visually sequence commercially produced paint colour charts from darkest to lightest of a given colour.
- Make cube lines. Using simple coloured cubes, create two identical sets of up to five cubes. Each cube should be a different colour. Give one set of cubes to the child and keep one set yourself. The child must not touch their cubes until told to do so. Sit opposite the child and place two cubes on the table in front of the child in a line. Ask the child to look at the cubes until they think they know the cubes used and their sequence. Then hide your cube set and ask the child to use their cubes to re-create your pattern. As the child correctly recalls the sequence, gradually increase the number of cubes used. If the child is struggling to recall the sequence try the following strategies:
  - articulate the sequence – '*Red is first and yellow is last*' – using appropriate language;
  - point to the cubes on either side of the child's midline.
- The previous activity could be developed using a Barrier Game approach. Two children sit facing each other with a screen between them so that they cannot see one another. They take turns in creating and describing a simple coloured cube sequence to their partner who must then construct the pattern.

Letter patterns

Teach the child to recall letter strings with two letters only.

- Create two-letter strings and words using magnetic letters. Use the same colours and different colours to differentiate the task.
- Create a matching game or Lotto with pairs of letters.
- Give plenty of practice of copying letter strings from models on same page.

49

Aspect 2: Visual sequential memory

Letter	Recognising and continuing patterns	Recognising and understanding serial order and associated vocabulary	Recalling multiple items in serial order	Recalling letter patterns
E	Recognises that patterns repeat	Understands concept of *first, second, third* ordinal position	Recalls two items with a change to a single attribute of size	Recalls letter in initial, medial or final position
E	Recognises two-step repeating pattern with a single attribute of colour	Uses conceptual language to talk about *first, second* and *third*	Recalls five items with a change to a single attribute of size	Recalls CVC word
F	Describes a simple two-step repeating pattern repeat	Can place self in *first, second* or *third* position in a line	Recalls two items with a change to a single attribute of left/right orientation	Recalls letters to construct a simple digraph
F	Copies two-step repeating pattern	Places self in position based on concept of ordinal number (e.g. *1st, 2nd, 3rd, 4th, 5th*)	Recalls three items with a change to a single attribute of left/right orientation	Recalls letters to construct simple tri-graph
G	Continues a pre-constructed two-step repeating pattern	Understands ordinal language used to denote position up to tenth place	Recalls four items with a change to a single attribute of left/right orientation	Recalls a single-syllable word with a single consonant preceding the vowel (e.g. *k-ing*)
G	Organises items into a two-step repeating pattern independently	Uses ordinal language to denote position up to *tenth* place	Recalls five items with a change to a single attribute of left/right orientation	Recalls a single-syllable word with two or three consonants preceding the vowel (e.g. *th-ing, str-ing*)

Suggested activities or strategies

Copying simple sequences

Teach the child to create simple sequencing patterns.

- Create sequencing patterns with children in the class. Base these sequences on, for example, hair colour, shoe colour, height, or making body shapes (e.g. hands up/hands down).
- Create repeating patterns of movement in PE
- Encourage children to mirror each other's pattern of movement.
- Use a range of objects to print a simple sequence pattern.

Order, order!!

Teach the child to order a range of familiar items and use ordinal language appropriately.

- Create simple races (e.g. by cars rolling down a slope). Discuss ordinal position.
- 'Go shopping'. Give the child a simple visual shopping list of three items that they must remember in order to help themselves retrieve the items in the correct order, without reference to the list.
- Place a range of objects next to a suitcase. Make a picture list for the child to look at briefly before they then pack the case in the correct order.
- Prepare some simple worksheets on which objects are seen in a line (e.g. a row of Christmas lights, or people wearing hats). Encourage the child to '*Colour the fourth hat red*' or '*Colour the eighth light yellow*'.
- The child follows a simple three-step visual sequence of getting a teddy ready for bed: putting on pyjamas/brushing its teeth/putting it to bed.

Remembering one thing

Teach the child to recall a range of simple objects in serial order, tracking from left to right, where there is a difference in orientation.

- Encourage the child to copy patterns of cups arranged so that handles are on the left or right or the object itself is facing left/right.

This could also be achieved using umbrellas, gloves, shoes, toy cars, paper arrows, teddy bears and so on.

Remembering words

Teach the child to recall a sequence of letters or phonemes. This task can be adapted by using a combination of tall and short letters (*huk, him*), short height and hanging (*gog, yop*) or a mixture of tall, short and hanging (*hing, quolp*).

- Draw a set of coloured chalk circles on the floor. Write a letter, phoneme or digit in each circle. Show the child a letter, letter string or nonsense word. The child must then go and stand in the circles that represent the sequence of letters shown (e.g. *fl-u-m-p*).
- Use coloured phoneme cards or magnetic letters to reproduce words shown on cards. Show one word at a time to the child. Can they read the word and reproduce it from memory, using magnetic letters or phoneme cards?
- Play Letter Phoneme Rainbows. Sit opposite the child and place a set of letter/phoneme cards in front of them. Place them carefully so that they are clearly organised on the child's left, at their body midline and on their right. Turn them over one card at a time from the left. The child must initially remember each letter as it has been turned. This task can then be differentiated by turning over more than one card at a time to be recalled in sequence until eventually all cards are turned and the child recalls the sequence at the end. Additionally, the cards could be colour coded individually or in groups.
- Encourage the child to recall words and letter strings through a Look, Say, Cover, Write, Check sequence.
- Word-building. Teach the child to construct words by placing a set of cards in order, where each card has another letter from the word or letter string added, e.g. *s–ing, st–ing, stri–ing, str–ing–y*.

51

Aspect 2: Visual sequential memory

Letter	Recognising and continuing patterns	Recognising and understanding serial order and associated vocabulary	Recalling multiple items in serial order	Recalling letter patterns
H	Recognises a simple three-step repeating pattern with apparatus	Copies a sequence of items correctly in the first, medial and last position on request	Recalls two items and attributes simultaneously (e.g. colour and shape)	Recalls a single-syllable non-word accurately
H	Copies a simple three-step repeating pattern with apparatus	Copies a sequence of up to ten items on request	Recalls two items and three attributes simultaneously (e.g. colour, shape and size)	Recalls a single-syllable word accurately
I	Continues a simple three-step repeating pattern with apparatus	Correctly names which item is in each ordinal position (*first, second, third*)	Recalls three items in serial order with two attributes of shape and colour	Recalls a simple two-syllable non-word accurately
I	Organises items into a three-step repeating pattern independently	Correctly recalls which item is in each ordinal position (*first, second, third*)	Recalls three items in serial order with three attributes of shape, size and colour	Recalls a simple two-syllable word accurately
J	Recognises a simple five-step repeating pattern with apparatus	Constructs own sequence of up to three items and correctly recalls items in each position	Recalls up to four items in serial order with attribute of shape and colour	Recalls a compound word accurately
J	Continues and explains simple five-step repeating patterns with apparatus	Creates a sequence with a number of items between three and ten	Recalls up to four items in serial order with three attributes of shape, size and colour	Recalls two related words accurately (e.g. *chewing gum*)

Suggested activities or strategies

Recognising complex patterns

Teach the child to recognise and continue sequences with up to five steps (e.g. knife, fork, spoon, cup, plate, knife, fork, spoon, cup, plate).

- Create patterns with familiar objects.
- Use peg boards to create patterns for the child and for the child to construct their own patterns.
- Use bead threading to create patterns with the child (red, blue, green, orange, yellow, red, blue, green, orange, yellow).

First, next, last

Teach the child to construct a three-step sequence from left to right given additional items.

- Work with the child to create and photograph simple three-step sequences from everyday classroom routines (e.g. take off coat, hang it on peg, sit down).
- Encourage the child to sequence a set of three simple process photographs (e.g. cook tea, eat tea, wash up).
- Photograph simple three-step routes around the building (e.g. line up in the classroom, go along the corridor, go out into the playground).
- Make simple obstacle course sequences.
- Order pictures of scenes from a nursery rhyme or familiar poem.
- Provide opportunities for the child to play with items and organise them into ordinal positions (e.g. toy cars or small world figures having a race). This task can be differentiated by using items that are either related or unrelated.

Remembering everything

Teach the child to construct multi-step repeating patterns. The complexity of this task should be increased by adding increasing numbers of variables to the sequencing items (e.g. colour/size/shape/pattern). For example, small red square, big blue triangle, medium yellow circle, big green oval, small orange star, small red square, big blue triangle, medium yellow circle, big green oval, small orange star.

- Create gummed paper shape patterns.
- Create patterns with 2D plane shapes.

Pretty poly

Teach the child to recall two-syllable words and two-word combinations.

- Use a variety of word to picture matching games (e.g. picture of chewing gum on one card and the words on a separate card).
- Colour-code syllables and digraphs/trigraphs on flash cards.
- Word/Picture Sums. Give the child a picture of a bed with the word *bed* written below and a picture of a room with the word *room* written below. Ask the child to put them together so they make sense – *bedroom*. Allow the child to look at the words for a given amount of time or until they know them. Remove them from view and the child must find the full version of the word (*bedroom*) from a selection of compound words. This activity can also be played in reverse, where the child is given the compound word to look at and then must find the parts.

53

Aspect 2: Visual sequential memory

Letter	Recognising and continuing patterns	Recognising and understanding serial order and associated vocabulary	Recalling multiple items in serial order	Recalling letter patterns
K	Recognises a multi-step repeating pattern independently	Responds correctly to questions regarding five-step sequences in order to recall which item is in *first* position	Recalls up to five line-drawn items in serial order with attributes of shape and colour	Copies single-syllable words/non-words from model in close proximity (on page and then from personal whiteboard)
K	Continues a multi-step repeating pattern independently	Responds correctly to questions regarding five-step sequences in order to recall which item is in *second* position	Recalls up to five line-drawn items in serial order with attributes of shape, size and colour	Copies simple sentence from model in direct view (personal whiteboard)
L	Continues a printed multi-step repeating pattern independently	Responds correctly to questions regarding five-step sequences in order to recall which item is in *final* position	Recalls up to five plain line-drawn symbols	Copies simple sentence from model in near distance (group whiteboard)
L	Constructs a multi-step repeating pattern using printed shapes	Responds correctly to questions regarding five-step sequences in order to recall which item is in any position	Recalls up to five similar plain line-drawn symbols	Copies simple sentence from model in further distance (class whiteboard)
M	Draws own simple repeating pattern	Recalls two items and their position in a five-step sequence	Recalls up to five similar plain line-drawn symbols with changes to size only	Copies complex sentence from model in near distance (group whiteboard)
M	Draws own complex repeating pattern	Recalls up to five items and their position in a five-step sequence	Recalls up to five similar plain line-drawn symbols with changes to size and orientation	Copies complex sentence from model in further distance (class whiteboard)

Suggested activities or strategies

Building and drawing patterns

Teach the child to construct multiple-step repeating patterns.

- Create a simple class washing line and encourage the child to create patterns by pegging items on the line.
- Provide the child with a range of pictured wrapping paper and encourage the child to cut and paste patterns.
- Provide drawing stencils/stampers and allow the child to construct patterns.

Recalling position

Teach the child to recall items in named positions.

- Use toy cars to create a sequential traffic jam or roll cars down a slope in order to discuss their sequential position.
- Play bug queues. Provide the child with a tub of plastic creatures. There are some useful commercially available tubs of coloured creatures, in which each bug is a different colour (e.g. spider = blue, grasshopper = orange, fly = yellow). Begin by helping the child make a bug queue and as you place each bug verbally label its position – *first*, *second*, *third*, *fourth*, *fifth* and so on. Then gather the bugs together and ask the child to place the bugs back in their correct position. This task can be made more simple by recalling only obviously different items, or more complex by recalling items from the same category or by recalling increasing numbers of creatures. Begin by using two items and increase with one item at a time. Ask the child to look at the creatures until they think they know them.
- Create a sequence of bugs as before. Ask the child to look away while you remove a bug. The child must then look back and recall:
  - which bug was removed;
  - the colour of the bug;
  - the position of the bug in the queue.

Symbol eyes

Teach the child to recall a sequence of simple symbols.

- Wingdings. Use the word-processing font Wingdings to create sequences of simple symbols for the child to recall.
- Provide the child with a simple code (e.g. a = ☆, b = ○, c = △). Can the child recall and sequence the letters, having been given the symbol sequence?

Total recall

Teach the child to copy from a variety of distances.

- Begin by allowing the child to copy from your written model on the page. The child copies beneath. Provide a set of coloured felt tip pens. The child can copy a pattern comprising a series of:
  - colours (coloured spots);
  - shapes (single-colour or different-coloured block shapes, outlined shapes of the same colour or different colours);
  - symbols (block- coloured or coloured outline);
  - letters.
- Then try the same activity from a personal whiteboard.
- Try the same activity from a group whiteboard.
- Try the same activity from the whole-class whiteboard.

Aspect 3: Visual closure

Letters	Guessing an object from parts	Dividing larger objects to find smaller parts	Building larger objects from smaller parts	Letters, syllables and words
A	Differentiates between an object that has one part (ball) and an object that has many parts (computer)	Demonstrates an organised visual attention search, stopping to direct gaze at specific items (top to bottom/left to right and so on)	Places piece in inset puzzle (5+) pieces	Identifies letter from dashed outline
A	Understands that objects may be made of parts and can name one part (e.g. part of a shoe)	Points to specific named parts	Places pieces and completes inset puzzle	Identifies letter from dotted outline
B	Names a variety of parts of a familiar object (e.g. person = hand, arm, shoulder)	Disassembles items (e.g. a Lego® model)	Uses bricks to build a tower	Cuts up a word to find constituent letters
B	Given an image, can identify key features of an object (e.g. an elephant has a trunk)	Disassembles items to find or sort parts (e.g. disassembles a simple Lego model to find number of bricks used)	Copies a simple brick tower	Cuts up a word to find constituent letter strings
C	Given images, can identify an item from multiple parts (e.g. whiskers, tail, paws = cat)	Cuts up a whole picture into halves then re-creates the picture	Copies a simple disconnected brick pattern using three bricks	Guesses a range of CVC words when letters are arranged in correct order, but spaced at onset/rime border
C	Identifies which part is missing when given the remainder of the object	Cuts up a whole picture into thirds then re-creates the picture	Copies a disconnected brick pattern using six bricks	Guesses a range of CVC words when letters are arranged in correct order but spaced C–V–C
D	Identifies item from a single directly identifiable part (e.g. a milkshake cup from its straw)	Cuts up a whole picture into quarters then re-creates the picture	Copies simple connected brick pattern using three bricks	Guesses CVC word when letters are presented one at a time (e.g. *c-a-t*)
D	Recognises a picture as pieces are provided one at a time	Cuts up a picture and matches parts to original image	Copies connected brick pattern using six bricks	Recognises CVC words from dotted and dashed outlines

Suggested activities or strategies

Bits and pieces

Teach the child to recognise that an object may be made of more than one part.

- Brainstorm picture features. Give the child a picture of an object or animal. Begin by naming a single feature, such as a long neck. Encourage the child to name as many features as they can see.
- What's that? Give the child a set of picture cards of items that belong to a specific item such as a car: steering wheel, tyre, seat, headlight and so on. Encourage the child to guess the object from the parts.
- Play odd part out. Give the child a set of part cards and add an incorrect part that does not belong to the group. Encourage the child to guess which card you have added to the group.
- Look at photographs of parts of an object. Is the child able to identify these parts on a 3D object?

Taking it apart

Teach the child to recognise that whole objects/images may be disassembled to find the constituent pieces.

- Lego® models. Give the child a simple Lego model and ask them to take it apart and sort it into its constituent blocks. Before they start, they must guess how many blocks they might have at the end (two, four, six?) and the respective colours. They could make a table of their guesses.
- Lego model pictures. As above, but remove the brick models and ask the children to guess from simple photos or line drawings how many bricks of each size there may be.
- Exploding shapes and pictures. During art or DT provide the child with coloured paper and 2D shapes. Allow the child to draw around and cut out the shapes. They should then dissect the shape into strips or interesting shapes and reassemble them on a large background sheet so that there are small spaces between each part but the shape is essentially identifiable.
- Colouring. Provide regular opportunities to complete simple colouring pictures.

Building block patterns

Teach the child to copy simple brick patterns. Begin with blocks that are not connected and work towards connected block patterns.

- Teach the child to copy a simple pattern of blocks from a 2D image. To begin with these should be arrangements of bricks in simple patterns. Then work towards more complicated joined structures using up to six blocks to create a simple 1/2/3 block staircase. Provide opportunities where you have constructed most of the pattern but omitted one or two bricks and covered these on the 2D plan. Child should place the bricks in the correct place using the plan.

Seeing small words

Teach the child to break/build CVC words.

- Provide plenty of opportunities for the child to complete letters by joining dots.
- Shredded words. Allow the child to cut words into phonemes and to paste them apart: $d - o - g$. The child could make a picture with a range of simple words of a variety of colours and fonts, shredded and pasted.
- Unroll a word. Arrange the letters/phonemes of a word and glue them in order along a piece of paper left to right. Roll the paper up so that the word can be revealed one letter or phoneme at a time for the child to build and predict the word.
- Missing letters in words. Provide regular opportunities for the child to predict letters missing from words, when given a picture clue. Begin with CVC words and single letter sounds.

57

Aspect 3: Visual closure

Letter	Guessing an object from parts	Dividing larger objects to find smaller parts	Building larger objects from smaller parts	Letters, syllables and words
E	Cuts up a whole picture into halves horizontally, vertically and/or diagonally then recreates the picture	Takes apart a four- to six-piece puzzle and talks about the removed parts	Matches vertical image halves of single item (e.g. table lamp)	Identifies initial letter of CVC word from dashed outline
E	Cuts up a whole picture into thirds then recreates the picture	Finds a specific piece of a four- to six-piece puzzle from an image	Matches horizontal image halves of single item	Identifies missing letters beyond rime border in CVC words from a dashed outline
F	Cuts up a whole picture into quarters then recreates the picture	Takes apart a six- to nine-piece puzzle and talks about the removed parts	Matches vertical image halves containing multiple items (e.g. view of garden)	Recognises missing phoneme in single-syllable word from a dashed outline
F	Cuts up a picture and matches parts to original image then recreates the picture	Finds a specific piece in a six- to nine-piece puzzle from an image	Matches horizontal image halves containing multiple items	Recognises single-syllable words from dotted and dashed outlines
G	Identifies a picture theme from up to five parts of the image then recreates the picture	Takes apart a 12-piece puzzle and talks about the removed parts	Can complete a simple picture cut in half vertically	Guesses two-syllable words when letters/phonemes are presented one at a time (e.g. *l-oo-k-i-ng*)
G	Identifies a picture theme from two image parts then recreates the picture	Finds a specific piece in a 12-piece puzzle from an image	Can complete a simple picture cut in half horizontally	Identifies missing letter combinations from their dashed outlines

Suggested activities or strategies

Picture perfect

Teach the child to see a picture from the sum of its parts. During art lessons give plenty of experience of cutting up pictures of landscapes, buildings and so on in a range of orientations (e.g. vertical cuts/horizontal cuts/diagonal cuts). The child should space the pieces and glue them down so the image can still be seen but pieces are spread apart.

Matching parts

Teach the child to find specific parts within a whole image.

- Use commercially produced jigsaw puzzles. Encourage the child to take apart simple jigsaws that you have put together, placing the pieces on their corresponding parts of the box lid picture. Encourage them to find specific pieces.
- Copy a simple image twice. Draw a 3×2 grid over both images. Give one image to the child and cut one image up along the grid lines. Give the child one cut part at a time to match with their grid image.

Matching halves

Teach the child to identify or 'notice' relevant details of single objects/pictures and to complete symmetrical parts and non-symmetrical parts.

- Complete magazine pictures by finding missing halves or quarters or parts of it.
- Give the child half of a picture. Use a range of orientations – cut the pictures vertically, horizontally, diagonally top left to bottom right, or bottom right to top left. Encourage the child to use a variety of art materials to create the missing half of the image.
- Provide regular opportunities for symmetrical pattern-making on squared paper. Use one or more line(s) of symmetry. Provide mirrors to help the child imagine the missing symmetrical parts.

Guess the word

Teach the child to 'close' words by combining letters/phonemes and words from their broken outlines.

- Building words. Allow the child to 'close' words from letters/phonemes. Divide words into letters/phonemes. Spread the constituent parts of the word with space between the letters and phonemes and ask the child to guess the word (e.g. *sh – ou – t*). Arrange these in relation to the child's body midline – place the medial sound/phoneme in the midline position.
- Use games containing word tiles. Provide opportunities to complete words using given letters and phonemes.
- Guess the letter/phoneme. Prepare a large set of letters/phonemes in different colours. You will also need to create a set of transparent overlays that contain either a wide thick vertical or horizontal or diagonal grid. Place the letter/phoneme underneath the overlay. This will mask off parts of the letter or phoneme. The thicker the grid lines, the less of the letter/phoneme the child will see. The child should visually 'close' and guess the hidden letter.
- Over-writing. The child has to guess a letter/phoneme from its broken outline and over-trace it.
- Disappearing letters. Write letters, phonemes and words onto a whiteboard with a whiteboard pen. Erase parts of letters in a range of orientations for the child to 'close' and guess the letters/phonemes/words.
- Match dashed letters/phonemes and words to their full lined versions.

Aspect 3: Visual closure

Letter	Guessing an object from parts	Dividing larger objects to find smaller parts	Building larger objects from smaller parts	Letters, syllables and words
H	Identifies an object from 75% view	Remembers content of parts removed from whole	Chooses correct piece from choice of two to complete a puzzle picture/model	Matches object to its outline or shadow
H	Identifies an object from 50% view	Using incomplete whole, can find removed part from among a group of distractors	Chooses piece to complete image from a choice of three	Matches tall or short letter to large or small box and fits two-letter words into tall/short or short/tall outlines (e.g. *to*, *at*)
I	Identifies an object from partial 25% view	Predicts content of missing part using context of whole	Chooses two pieces to complete an image from a choice of up to six pieces	Fits words containing tall and short height letters to their outline (e.g. *lie*, *will*)
I	Identifies an object from a random isolated part	Identifies context from missing parts to the image (e.g. bucket, seagull = seaside)	Chooses two pieces to complete an image from a choice of up to 12 pieces	Fits words containing short-height and hanging letters to their outline (e.g. *cap*, *pin*)
J	Completes/closes the simple broken outline of a circle	Predicts resulting part when object is cut in half (e.g. a square cut diagonally will produce a triangle)	Completes half of a puzzle	Fits words containing tall, short and hanging letters to their outline (e.g. *shopping*)
J	Closes a simple line-drawn shape with one side omitted (e.g. draws the fourth side of a square)	Predicts resulting parts when a picture of an object cut into quarters (e.g. home = roof/upstairs/downstairs/garden)	Completes three-quarters of a puzzle	Suggests letters/phonemes missing from outline of words

Suggested activities or strategies

One at a time

Teach the child to identify an image from random information provided.

- Spinner picture. Cut a piece of card into 6, 9 or 12 squares that will form a grid covering an image. Number each piece. Use a spinner. The child spins the spinner and removes the corresponding numbered piece of card. The child must guess the picture as quickly as possible.
- Picture strips. Cut pictures into vertical or horizontal strips and encourage the child to paste the pieces into place one piece at a time and guess the picture.
- Cut a small window out of an A4 piece of card. Use a variety of window shapes and vary the percentage size of the aperture to differentiate the task. Place the 'window card' in front of an A4 picture so that only part may be seen through the window. The child must guess the image theme. Also prepare a window aperture as above but use a window card that is larger than the image so that the window may be moved around the image.
- Whiteboard fun. Draw simple plane shapes on a whiteboard, then erase parts of the shapes (e.g. one side of a square) and ask the child to draw these parts back in.
- Use the 'spotlight' tool in computer programmes to mask all of a picture except for the highlighted part. Move the spotlight around the image and ask the child to guess what the picture shows.

What was that?

Teach the child to recall missing parts of images.

- Lost jigsaw pieces. Allow child to look carefully at the picture on the box lid of the jigsaw and then remove the image. Remove one or two pieces from the corresponding completed puzzle and encourage the child to recall what was shown in that part of the image.
- Puzzle search. Ask the child to match jigsaw pieces to their place on the jigsaw box lid.

Puzzles and pieces

Teach the child to recognise parts that are relevant and/or irrelevant.

- Jigsaw puzzles. Allow the child plenty of practice completing simple jigsaw puzzles but 'back chain' the task by removing only one piece at first. Then encourage the child to replace increasing numbers of missing pieces in ready-made jigsaw puzzles. Each time, ask the child to identify the part of the image where the piece has been removed and the content of that image part.
- Jigsaw puzzles. Work with the child to build jigsaw puzzles of increasing numbers of pieces.
- Double puzzles. Create two separate puzzle pictures cut into their constituent parts. Begin by asking the child to look at the puzzle pictures to identify parts that they will be searching for. Jumble the pieces together. Encourage the child to identify pieces that do or do not belong to each of the puzzles and to sort and complete each puzzle.

What's missing?

Teach the child to recognise words from their outlines.

- Revisit the child's ability to complete inset puzzles independently.
- Outlines. Teach the child to match the word to its outline shape. Differentiate this task by using a clear variety of letters to begin with (tall, short, hanging). Work towards less obvious combinations.
- Missing letters. Provide the child with words within their shape outlines. Remove letters or digraphs and encourage the child to choose from a possible range of letters and digraphs that would make known words.

- Scrabble®. Play Scrabble to identify letters that would contribute to create known words. There are junior versions of this game available.

Aspect 3: Visual closure

Letter	Guessing an object from parts	Dividing larger objects to find smaller parts	Building larger objects from smaller parts	Letters, syllables and words
K	Identifies and completes a dot-to-dot of a regular shape (e.g. a hexagon)	Identifies what's missing from a known object	When shown a 3D model, predicts bricks required for construction	Cuts up sentence to find individual words
K	Identifies and completes an irregular shape dot-to-dot	Identifies what's missing from a scene	Chooses and organises bricks to form a whole	Combines individual words to construct sentences
L	Identifies and completes a simple dot-to-dot picture	Identifies what's wrong with an object – a visual absurdity (e.g. a cup with no handle)	Uses bricks to build a model with three stages (e.g. fuselage, tail, wings = aeroplane)	Predicts missing words from sentence using the preceding words
L	Identifies and completes a complex dot-to-dot picture	Identifies what's wrong with a scene – a visual absurdity (e.g. tennis player has no racket)	Uses bricks to build a model with four stages	Predicts missing words from sentence using the following words
M	Completes a simple colour-by-numbers	Finds a letter in a word search grid	Uses bricks to build a model with multiple stages	Highlights different sentences in a short text passage
M	Guesses an image hidden in a simple colour-by-numbers	Finds a word in a word search grid	Uses bricks to build a model with multiple stages and parts	Predicts missing words in a paragraph

Suggested activities or strategies

Dot-to-dots

Teach the child to close and recognise a range of simple to complex dot-to-dot pictures.

- Use coloured rubber floor spots. Encourage the child to follow a trail of these markers and then return to their starting position.
- Geoboards. Allow the child to explore shapes that can be made using a geoboard and elastic bands.
- Plastic stencils. Provide regular access to plastic picture stencils, where the child draws through the spaces to create a simple shape.
- Complete partial picture outlines.
- Train tracks. Use curved and straight pieces to make track combinations.
- Draw shapes on dotted paper.
- Pegboards. Provide opportunities for the child to complete pegboard patterns. Begin by leaving out every other peg and gradually increase the number missing (e.g. omit an entire side from a square).
- Dot-to-dots. Provide regular opportunities to complete a range of dot-to-dots.

What's wrong?

Teach the child to identify what is missing from a given image (e.g. spots missing from a ladybird). The child should also be encouraged to identify items that are not relevant to the context, such as someone placing a cake to bake in a washing machine.

- Play heads and tails. There are a number of published 'Misfit' games and books. Alternatively, choose a range of pictures and cut them all in half along the same orientation to create a top and bottom that may be interchanged (e.g. the top of an ice cream and the legs of a table). Allow the child to play by mixing up tops and bottoms. Encourage the child to predict what is missing and would be needed to complete each jumbled item (e.g. the cone of the ice cream).
- Sliding window. Place an A4 image in a plastic file pocket with a piece of card on top so that when the card is pulled from the pocket the picture will be revealed from the top of the image. Slowly pull the card out of the plastic pocket, thereby slowly revealing the image from the top. The child must guess as quickly as possible the content of the image.
- Use commercial or online 'What's wrong?' pictures. Encourage the child to identify and explain visual absurdity by identifying what is wrong in a picture (e.g. the boy is fishing with a violin).

Brick building

Teach the child to build simple brick models, imagining the 'look' of the final model as they go.

- Provide regular opportunities for the child to build a model from a 2D photograph.
- Build brick walls in which each course is different. Each course could be a single colour, but the task can be differentiated by making each course of bricks contain a variety of colours.
- Provide opportunities to follow brick model-building instructions, where the model instructions are visually sequenced.

Words and sentences

Teach the child to isolate words in sentences.

- Highlighters. Provide the child with a highlighter pen. Ask the child to choose a target word and to highlight it as many times as it appears in a copied piece of text. (This can also be encouraged for specific phonemes and sounds.)
- Favourite books. Copy a sentence from the child's favourite book. Encourage the child to paint a picture illustrating an event from the book that is represented by the sentence. The sentence can then be cut up and hidden round the picture to be found and read in order. Extend this task by writing, cutting up and hiding more than one sentence. To ensure that each sentence is more easily identified, write each sentence in a different colour.
- Cloze procedure. Provide regular opportunities for the child to complete cloze procedure tasks, in which words are missing from the text and must be predicted or chosen from lists in separate panels.

Letter	Identifying item attributes	Recognising and identifying item changes	Identifying, comparing and making the same (matching/ordering)	Discriminating letters and sounds
A	Uses language *is, is not* to describe an object	Understands concept of not the same (different)	Understands concept of the same	Finds a lower-case letter on request
A	Uses language *has, has not* to describe an object	Names two items that are different	Names two items that are identical	Matches lower-case magnetic letter to image
B	Is able to identify the basic concept of colour	Compares two items to identify a single key difference	Finds two similar items from a group	Matches lower-case short letters: *s, i, a, n*
B	Is able to identify the basic concept of size	Identifies two differences between two items	Compares single items to identify a single key similarity	Matches lower-case short letters: *s, i, a, n, m, o, c, e, u, i*
C	Is able to identify the basic concept of shape	Identifies multiple differences between two items	Identifies key similarities between two items	Matches lower-case tall letters: *t, d, k*
C	Is able to identify the basic concept of position/orientation – discriminates between left and right	Identifies subtle differences between two items	Identifies key similarities between items in a small group	Matches lower-case tall letters: *t, d, k, h, b, f, l*
D	Is able to identify basic concepts of number	Compares multiple items to identify a single difference	Matches two identical items	Matches lower-case letters which are hanging: *g, p*
D	Is able to identify basic concepts of pattern	Compares multiple items to identify multiple differences	Matches items on the basis of colour	Matches lower-case letters which are hanging: *g, p, j, q, y*

Suggested activities or strategies

Basic concepts

Teach the child basic conceptual vocabulary with which to describe objects.

- Use paint colour charts to match and name colours.
- Provide regular opportunities for the child to categorise items, such as shapes.
- Provide a box of items for the child to play with that are organised to teach a specific concept, such as a range of toys of different colours. Allow the child to play with them but give a running commentary on their actions and the items ensuring that you use appropriate vocabulary to describe the objects: '*You are bouncing the* **red** *ball*'.
- In PE, perform movement patterns involving *left* and *right*.
- Play Simon Says and include instructions using number, *left*, *right*, and so on.

Spot the difference

Teach the child to identify single differences between objects and multiple differences between a range of items.

- Use traditional 'Spot the difference' activities. Consider differentiating this task by:
  - beginning with differences identifiable between two single items;
  - using images where the items to be compared are horizontally aligned and where they are vertically aligned;
  - using single images against a background;
  - working towards more complex scenes with additional detail;
  - differentiating by using black and white/colour activities.

Matching items

Teach the child to match a group of items.

- Teach the child to match a basket full of jumbled socks or pairs of shoes in the correct orientation.
- Match pairs of toys of a range of sizes.
- Snap. Play this traditional card game by taking turns to place one card each face up. If the cards match, shout '*Snap*'. The first person to shout '*Snap*' collects those two cards and the winner is the player with the most cards when all cards have been paired. If the cards do not match, the players continue to simultaneously place cards until two matching cards appear. Regularly direct the child's attention to the cards being 'the same' or 'different'.
- Cut items from old shop catalogues for the child to match.
- Match photographs of class members with other photographs of them in a class photograph.

Lower-case lookout

Teach the child to discriminate between lower-case letters.

- Match magnetic letters.
- Create a vertical line of random lower-case letters on the left-hand side of an A4 page. Create a corresponding but mixed list of lower-case letters on the right of the page. The child must then match a letter from the left to its counterpart on the right.
- Paint a range of lettering.
- Play Letter Dominoes.
- Hunt the letter. Provide a page of lower-case letters, some of which are the target letter and some of which are distractors. Encourage the child to find the target letters on the page.

Aspect 4: Visual discrimination

Letter	Identifying item attributes	Recognising and identifying item changes	Identifying, comparing and making the same (matching/ordering)	Discriminating letters and sounds
E	Identifies one key feature of an item (e.g. bike = wheels)	Can name things that change, from personal experience	Compares multiple items to identify a single similarity	Identifies which letters have curved edges
E	Identifies more than one feature of a single item	Understands concept of change and can make a change to an object	Compares multiple items to identify multiple similarities	Identifies which letters have straight edges
F	Identifies an item of a given colour	Can make a change to a group of objects	Matches items on the basis of size	Identifies which letters have a combination of straight and curved edges
F	Identifies an item of a given size/shape	Identifies a simple change to a single item (e.g. apple is now red rather than green)	Matches items on the basis of shape	Sorts letters into groups: curved, straight, straight and curved edges
G	Identifies an item of a given orientation	Recognises a change to physical appearance of a familiar person	Matches items on the basis of position/ orientation	Identifies which letters have straight edges on left or right-hand edge/ top or bottom
G	Finds items with common features (e.g. finds everything with wheels)	Recognises a change to physical appearance of a less familiar person	Matches items on the basis of quantity	Identifies which letters have curved edges on left or right-hand edge/ top or bottom

Suggested activities or strategies

Have or have not?

Teach the child to identify relevant detail.

- Picture clues. Provide the child with themed pictures (e.g. depicting a visit to the seaside). The child should dictate a list of the items in the picture that are related to the theme, such as *bucket*, *spade*, *sand*.
- Teach the concept of 'important', drawing the child's attention to what is relevant in what the child sees. The child could ring items that are important in a picture. Alternatively, provide the child with a digital camera and ask them to photograph ten important items related to an object or place.
- Brainstorm. Look at an object and brainstorm all the things that are associated with that specific object (e.g. car = wheels, tyres, steering wheel).

Changeabout

Teach the child to understand the concept of change.

- Make a collage of changes (e.g. seasons/life cycles).
- Look through books about opposites.
- Odd one out. Prepare or download a sheet displaying a row of objects that are identical in respect of size, shape or colour with one object that is different. Encourage the child to find the odd object out. To differentiate this task use sets of objects that are the same/different in more than one aspect of size, colour or shape.
- Play dressing-up games and Guess Who?

Similarities

Teach the child to compare items in order to identify key similarities.

- Provide plenty of opportunities for sorting activities.
- Explore photos of family and look for similarities and likenesses and/or look at pictures of people from magazines to find similarities. Differentiate this task by asking the child to find similar faces among increasing numbers of faces.
- Play Lotto games.
- Match pictures to their shadows.
- Play Pelmanism (matching) games. Use picture pair cards. Place them face up and encourage the child to match the picture pairs.
- Play Picture and Number Dominoes. Play this game in the traditional manner whereby each child takes a turn to place their dominoes with one of its sides matching the free side of dominoes already placed.

Letter shapes

Teach the child to recognise the difference between curves and straight edges.

- Feely bag. Place a range of wooden or plastic letters in a feely bag. The child must feel the letter without looking, and describe whether the letter has curved, straight, or both curved and straight sides. Differentiate this task by showing an image of the letter while the child is feeling for the letter.
- Provide opportunities to paint letters and make letters out of salt dough.
- Provide the child with large photocopied letters and a set of Wikki-Stix® or pipecleaners. The child should use them to make the letter by following the photocopy outline.
- Use form boards. The child sorts a variety of letters into their corresponding spaces.

Aspect 4: Visual discrimination

Letter	Identifying item attributes	Recognising and identifying item changes	Identifying, comparing and making the same (matching/ordering)	Discriminating letters and sounds
H	Finds an item at top, middle or bottom of an image	Recognises a change of colour	Sorts items on the basis of colour	Identifies and sorts lower-case letters
H	Finds an item in the left/right of an image	Recognises a change of size	Sorts items on the basis of size	Identifies and sorts upper-case letters
I	Finds an item of given colour in an image	Recognises a change of shape	Sorts items on the basis of shape	Discriminates between upper-case and lower-case letters
I	Finds an item of given size in an image	Recognises a change of position	Sorts items on the basis of orientation	Identifies letters which are short (e.g. *a, e, u*) from a mixture of short/tall/hanging
J	Finds an item of given shape in an image	Recognises a change of quantity	Sorts items on the basis of quantity	Identifies letters which are tall (e.g. *h, l, k*) from a mixture of short/tall/hanging
J	Finds an item of a given orientation in an image	Recognises a combination of attribute changes	Sorts items with a combination of attributes (e.g. finds all the blue spiders where there are a range of different coloured creatures)	Identifies letters which are hanging (e.g. *g, p, j*) from a mixture of short/tall/hanging

Suggested activities or strategies

Picture treasure hunt

Teach the child to find specific items in an image.

- Give regular opportunities to discuss the content of pictures in reading books.
- Use pictures to complete a 'treasure hunt'. For example, tell the child to '*Find something round*' or '*Find something that is white*' or '*Tell me what colour the car is*'.
- Cut pictures into thirds (top, middle and bottom) or halves (left/right) and play a game of I Spy (e.g. '*I Spy something in the middle of the picture beginning with b*').
- Use published 'search' books in which the child can, for example, find sea creatures in an undersea picture.

All change

Teach the child to spot multiple changes to similar pictures/scenes.

- Computer airbrushing. Use a digital camera to take a simple picture. Paste the photo into a digital image-enhancing package. Change aspects of the photo and print it alongside the original. Encourage the child to identify the changes.
- Use 'Spot the difference' games and puzzle books. Begin with black line drawings, and move onto photos and pictures in commercially produced packs.
- Use cards on which there are changing attributes to find, for example, a creature with long/short ears, that is blue/red, that has two/three eyes.

Sort it out

Teach the child to sort methodically and to focus on a specific characteristic.

- Sort by object, texture, colour, shape or picture. For example, sort a box of Lego bricks or a bag of buttons.

- Form boards. Children sort a variety of shapes into their corresponding spaces.
- Shape sorters. Children sort a variety of shapes into their corresponding holes.
- Sort buttons for size, colour, number of holes and so on. **(Please be aware of choking hazard and do not leave child unattended.)**
- Sort pencils for size.
- Sort Smarties/pom-poms for colour.
- Sort Lego bricks for colour, size, shape, numbers of holes and so on.
- Sort gloves/shoes into left/right.

Type-writer

Teach the child to discriminate between letter size and shape.

- Word outlines. The child matches words to their shape outlines.
- Match magnetic lower- and upper-case letters to printed examples of that letter.
- Make a set of letter dominoes. The child can place a lower-case letter if its corresponding upper-case letter is available.
- Letter detective. Hide lower-case and corresponding upper-case letters in a simple grid. The child colours the lower-case in one colour and the upper-case in another colour. Differentiate this task by increasing the size of the grid and the number of target letters.
- Provide the child with a word/sentence/paragraph and three highlighter pens – red, amber and green. Encourage the child to find and highlight a given number of tall (red), short (amber) and hanging (green) letters in a given time.
- Explore the relationship between letter sizes as you word-process different letters.

Aspect 4: Visual discrimination

Letter	Identifying item attributes	Recognising and identifying item changes	Identifying, comparing and making the same (matching/ordering)	Discriminating letters and sounds
K	Finds an item in vertical relation to other items in an image (e.g. finds the key below the lamp)	Identifies a single feature added to or removed from an object	Orders on the criteria of size	Matches CVC words with multiple phoneme differences (e.g. *can–can, cut–cut*)
K	Finds an item in horizontal relation to other items in an image (e.g. finds the key to the right of the lamp)	Identifies multiple features added to or removed from an object	Orders on the criteria of quantity	Matches single-syllable words with a single phoneme difference (e.g. *spring–spring, sprung–sprung* or *thing–thing, sting–sting*)
L	Finds an item in an image given a single attribute (e.g. finds a red ball)	Identifies object added to a group	Orders on the criteria of shade of colour: light to dark	Matches two-syllable words with a single phoneme difference (e.g. *singing–singing, sinking–sinking*)
L	Finds item in an image given two related attributes (e.g. finds a small red ball)	Identifies object removed from a group	Orders on the criteria of shade of colour: dark to light	Matches words on a given attribute (e.g. those beginning with *s* or containing the digraph *ow*)
M	Finds item in an image given three related attributes (e.g. finds a big red ball with a star)	Identifies multiple additional objects	Perceives same object against different backgrounds	Sorts words to identify those with letter changes
M	Finds a number of objects with a given attribute (e.g. finds all the arrows facing left)	Identifies multiple objects removed from a group	Recognises same object in different orientations against different visually complex backgrounds	Sorts words into pairs with minimal differences in letters (e.g. spring–string)

Suggested activities or strategies

Picture perfect treasure hunt

Teach the child to find specific items in specific positions in an image.

- Show the child a small cue picture of an item they must discriminate and find in the larger image.
- Create an overlay grid and teach the child to look methodically.
- Use images and play I Spy (e.g. '*I Spy the* **small red triangle**'. In this example you will need a range of shapes that are small and of different colours.
- Use the computer to copy and paste tools to create worksheets of similar shapes in different orientations.

More or less?

Teach the child to discriminate what is missing from or added to an object or group.

- Play Kim's Game. Provide the child with a selection of objects on a tray. Allow the child time to look at the tray before covering the items with a cloth. Remove an item from the tray out of the child's view. The child should then be allowed to look at the tray again and see if they can spot what has been changed.
- Use packs of commercial 'What's missing?' cards.

All sorted

Teach the child to order and grade items from the least to the most and from the most to the least.

- Use paint colour charts to order by colour shade/tint.
- During art lessons encourage the pupil to colour-mix tints, adding colour to white, and black to colour, to darken. Colour concentric rings to show progressive shades of colour.
- Order buttons, plates, shoes, modelling clay snakes, string, paper strips or people by size.
- Teach the child to order by quantity/capacity by using measuring jugs, spots on ladybirds, marbles in jars.

- During art lessons, teach isolating objects from a background, using painting activities to camouflage creatures on a background. Use ICT Paint programmes or Photoshop to cut out objects and paste them against a variety of backgrounds.
- Provide regular opportunities to complete colouring activities where the colouring spaces are demarcated with a single spot.

Odd words

Teach the child to identify simple differences between words.

- Letter change. Provide the child with a list of words and encourage them to identify the difference in each word (e.g. *pot, pat, pit* or *well, fell, bell*).
- Lotto. Play Lotto/Bingo where each child has to match word to word.
- Word searches. Prepare simple grid word searches where words have minimal differences (e.g. *jump/jumping/jumped/jumps*).
- Odd one out. Prepare a sheet with a row of words where all words are identical except one word that has a single letter change (e.g. *cat, cat, cat, can, cat, cat*). The child should identify which word is the odd one out.
- Peg it. Write sequences of letters onto wooden pegs. The child should then peg these onto cards with the identical letter or rime.
- Colour by letters/rimes/phonemes. Place letters or digraphs in a simple black and white line drawing with a colouring key for the child to colour in (e.g. l = red, t = blue, j = green).
- Invite children to sequence a set of words in order so that only one letter changes at a time (e.g. *top, tip, tin, pin, pit*).
- Give the child a set of sorting trays, each containing an initial letter or letter string, and a set of words that begin with these letters or contain these strings. The child must sort the words into the correct sorting tray.

Letter	Recognising and identifying same/ different in size, position and number	Recognising and identifying same/ different in rotation	Recognising and identifying same/ different in laterality	Recognising and identifying same/ different in vertical inversion
A	Identifies change in size	Understands the concept of rotation as it applies to turning self	Knows left hand	Knows and responds to language *up* in relation to self
A	Chooses an object that is of a different size	Understands the concept of rotation as it applies to objects	Knows right hand	Knows and responds to language *down* in relation to self
B	Knows if a given object is bigger than another object	Demonstrates the concept of clockwise rotation in self	Demonstrates an understanding of right laterality/direction as it relates to self (body midline) (e.g. puts something on the right/ turns to right)	Knows and responds to language *above* in relation to self
B	Knows if an object is smaller	Demonstrates concept of anticlockwise rotation in self	Demonstrates an understanding of left laterality/direction as it relates to self (body midline) (e.g puts something on the left/ turns to left)	Knows and responds to language *below* in relation to self
C	Identifies objects of similar/same size	Demonstrates concept of anticlockwise rotation in objects	Identifies left laterality in relation to a single object. Can say whether something is on the left side	Recognises when a photograph is upside down
C	Identifies objects of different size	Demonstrates concept of clockwise rotation in objects	Identifies right laterality in relation to a single object. Can say whether something is on the right side	Correctly orientates photograph
D	Sorts and discriminates large/small identical items	Recognises which person has rotated	Identifies aspects of a single object that fall within a right laterality (e.g. the thumb on this glove is on the right)	Given two objects, can say which one is correctly vertically organised
D	Sorts and discriminates large/medium/small identical items	Recognises which object has been rotated	Identifies aspects of a single object that fall within a left laterality (e.g. the leaf on this plant is on the left)	Given two objects, can say which one is incorrectly vertically organised

Suggested activities or strategies

Big or small?

Teach the child to discriminate object size.

- With younger children, use inset puzzles where pieces are arranged in order of size.
- Use 'Tower of Hanoi' to organise rings in size order.
- Use a set of Russian dolls and encourage the child to organise them.
- Encourage the child to help organise up to five members of the class in height order.
- Begin by encouraging the child to find and/or make objects that are bigger, the same size as and smaller than themselves.
- Give the child a tin of buttons to order according to size.
  (NOTE: **Choking hazard. This task must be supervised for safety to ensure that children do not put buttons in their mouth.**)
- Sort socks, balls, hoops, kitchen utensils, Lego bricks of various sizes.
- Use a simple ICT publishing programme for the child to create, copy and resize their own pictures and letters.

Turning around

Teach the child to understand, recognise and correctly perform rotation.

- Use a 'Lazy Susan'. Place this in the middle of the table. Encourage the child to choose an object to place on the Lazy Susan. The child should rotate the object and draw it from different angles.
- Use programmable toys. Initially, give simple instructions to turn to the left/right/clockwise/anticlockwise.
- Explore rotation of shapes in mathematics. Pin a shape in its centre and draw around its outline/perimeter, rotate the shape and draw around it again. Continue to rotate and trace around the shape to create a piece of artwork.
- Create colour-segmented spinners and write physical actions for the child to perform in each section (e.g. turn towards the window).

Which way round?

Teach the child to discriminate laterality (left/right).

- School badge. Teach left/right by identifying the side their school badge is on when they are wearing their school jumper.
- Place different coloured stickers on their left/right hand or inside their shoes.
- Simon Says. Play simple games of Simon Says but add left and right (e.g. '*Simon Says wave your right hand*').
- Barrier Game. Child sits facing a peer but with a barrier between them. The children take turns to describe to their friend how to place items on a simple grid, including *left/right* vocabulary.

Up or down?

Teach the child the concept of up/down/upside down.

- Cut pictures from magazines and make an upside-down picture.
- Make an upside-down and right-way-up display (e.g. stand teddies on their heads).
- Use ICT to vertically flip images and play with them.
- Play Guess the Object. Show the child pictures of items that are upside down. Can they guess what each object is?

Aspect 5: Visual form constancy

Letter	Identifying and recognising same/ different in size, position and number	Identifying and recognising same/ different in rotation	Identifying and recognising same/ different in laterality	Identifying and recognising same/ different in vertical inversion
E	Demonstrates understanding of conservation of number	Identifies and matches objects with similar rotation	Recognises and identifies any change in laterality	Recognises and identifies any change in vertical inversion
E	Demonstrates understanding of conservation of volume	Rotates objects to match item models	Identifies and matches objects of similar lateral orientation	Identifies and matches objects of similar vertical inversion
F	Identifies and makes a change in amount but understands that items remain the same	Rotates objects through a quarter turn on request	Sorts objects according to laterality (e.g. sorts everything pointing left together)	Sorts objects according to vertical inversion (e.g. sorts everything pointing up)
F	Identifies and makes a change in position but understands that items remain the same	Rotates objects through a half turn on request	Sorts objects according to laterality (e.g. sorts everything pointing right together)	Sorts objects according to vertical inversion (e.g. sorts everything pointing down)
G	Matches items for position and number but understands that items remain the same	Rotates objects through a three-quarter turn on request	Identifies odd one out according to lateral inversion (e.g. in a group of five objects pointing to the left, the child can find the one pointing to the right)	Identifies odd one out according to inversion (e.g. in a group of five objects pointing up, the child can find the one pointing down; or in a group of five trees the child can find the three that are orientated correctly
G	Identifies odd one out according to size, position or number	Rotates objects through one whole turn on request	Corrects laterality of odd one out	Corrects orientation of odd one out

Suggested activities or strategies

Matching position and number

Teach the child to match groups of items according to number and position of objects and ensure that they understand the conservation of number and volume.

- Explore brick tower patterns. Encourage the child to make a tower with coloured bricks and then to make a companion tower with the same coloured bricks but in different configurations or as a direct opposite.
- Play with/explore dominoes and playing cards in order to 'recognise' that numbers can have certain configurations, like 5 or 6 on a dice/playing card (subitising).
- Use finger painting and colouring spots to make creative art patterns. For example, tell the child that they may use five spots of each colour and can explore the different configuration/patterns they can create. This could also be achieved in Numeracy with squared paper. The child could explore the different patterns of 8 and so on.
- Play with and explore a range of capacity containers. Encourage the child to fill containers to look the same/look different.
- Place a selection of balls in different hoops for the child to match.
- Use barrier games. Two children face each other with a barrier between them. They take turns to give and receive instructions including information about the position and number of objects in a grid (e.g. *'Put two triangles in the top left square'*).

How far to turn?

Teach the child to turn objects around by varying amounts.

- Use commercially produced cog and gear games.
- Create and decorate spinners.
- Make a simple safe dial.
- Use programmable toys and encourage the child to observe programming to make them turn.

- Explore object rotation by placing object on a 'Lazy Susan' and drawing or photographing them.

Matches laterality

Teach the child to secure their understanding of laterality.

- Begin by teaching the child to physically identify their left and right side. Use two gloves, one left and one right, but make sure that the gloves are different colours (e.g. left = green, right = red). Play a simple game in which the child has to raise their hand or pick up an object with a specific hand when instructed.
- Construct a simple obstacle course where the child must navigate from commands given to travel forward/back/left/right.
- Give instructions to programmable toys so they travel left and right.
- Give the child a set of objects where there can be an obvious laterality (e.g. cups where the handle is either on the right or left). Place the cup with the handle in the chosen laterality and the child must then orientate their cups similarly.
- Use a simple ICT programme to create shapes and flip them horizontally. Encourage the child to identify matching pairs.

Upside down all sorted

Teach the child to find identically vertically orientated shapes.

- Give the child picture cards of objects viewed from unusual angles. Help the child to predict the object.
- Place objects in a feely bag upside down and help the child to visualise what they may be.
- Play Heads and Tails with coins.
- Create patterns with empty drinks cans. **(Note: discard any items with sharp edges.)**

Aspect 5: Visual form constancy

Letter	Identifying and recognising same/different in size, position and number	Identifying and recognising same/different in rotation	Identifying and recognising same/different in laterality	Identifying and recognising same/different in vertical inversion
H	Understands that when a shape is a different size, or in a different position, it remains the same shape	Demonstrates understanding and application of the concept of half and one whole rotation	Understands that when a shape is laterally inverted it remains the original shape	Understands that when a shape is vertically inverted it remains the original shape
H	Matches shapes of similar size	Demonstrates understanding and application of the concept of one quarter and three-quarter rotation	Can identify a simple straight-sided irregular shape from its lateral inversion	Can identify a simple straight-sided irregular shape from its vertical inversion
I	Identifies odd shape out according to size	Finds and orientates a regular plane shape to match the rotation of a given shape	Can identify a simple curved-sided irregular shape from its lateral inversion	Can identify a simple curved-sided irregular shape from its vertical inversion
I	Identifies shapes similar in size (e.g. finds all middle-sized triangles in in a row of triangles of different sizes)	Finds a simple irregular plane shape that matches model	Identifies and matches a laterally inverted shape within a group of three distractors	Identifies and matches a vertically inverted shape within a group of three distractors
J	Sorts identical shapes in order of size, large to small	Finds a simple straight-edged shape that matches rotation	Can laterally invert a simple shape	Can vertically invert a simple shape
J	Sorts identical shapes in order of size, small to large	Finds a simple curved-edged shape that matches model	Can laterally invert a complex shape	Can vertically invert a complex shape

Suggested activities or strategies

Size it up

Teach the child to identify changes of size. Begin by using a range of objects, then move towards identifying changes of size in 2D images of objects and finally in identifying size difference in letters.

- Use a range of objects where size can be made obvious to the child (e.g. pencils, shoes, teddies). Place a range of objects of the same size together. Place one object of a different size randomly between them. Ask the child to find the odd one out. This task may be differentiated by adding more items, more items that are the odd ones out, and by adding items of increasing visual complexity.
- Explore enlarging text/pictures by using word processing packages to specify sizes.

Rotation

Teach the child to recognise and create rotational movement.

- Provide the child with streamer sticks and allow the child to make patterns in the air, spinning and rotating. Draw a distinction between rotating clockwise and anticlockwise.
- Use a range of toy nuts and bolts to demonstrate and identify clockwise and anticlockwise rotation.
- Play with kaleidoscopes and rotate the barrels.
- Draw around a simple plane shape or object in a range of orientations. Provide the child with a set of identical shapes and encourage the child to match the shape to the outline.
- Play with and explore simple stencils by rotating the stencil.
- Cut out a cardboard shape. Put it in the centre of a piece of thick card. Draw around the shape. Rotate the shape and draw around again. Rotate the shape and draw around again. Repeat as required to create a rotational colouring pattern.
- Use a simple ICT word processing/publishing programme to create and rotate shapes or pictures of the child.

Odd directions

Teach the child to identify changes of laterality. Begin by using a range of objects and work towards recognising these changes in pictures and shapes.

- Use a range of objects where laterality can be made obvious to the child (e.g. gloves, shoes, cups, socks). Place a range of objects facing one direction and move one object or picture to face the opposing direction. The child should find the odd one out.
- Use tracing paper to copy over a simple picture with a soft lead pencil. Turn it to the left or right, place it face down on another piece of paper and rub over the back of the tracing. This should then transfer the image over onto the paper as a lateral inversion. (Avoid lettering or digits.)

Odd way up

Teach the child to identify vertical changes. Begin by using a range of objects and work towards 2D representations and finally shapes.

- Use tracing paper to copy over a simple picture with a soft lead pencil. Flip it vertically up or down, place face down on another sheet of paper and rub over the back of the tracing. This should then transfer the image onto the paper in vertical inversion. (Avoid lettering or digits.)
- Place a piece of paper in landscape orientation. Fold the piece of paper in half. Using black paint, paint a shape or object on the top half of the paper. Then fold the the paper over and rub gently on the back of the painted shape to transfer it as a vertical inversion onto the bottom half of the folded paper. Decorate.
- Use isometric paper and mirrors if required to create inverted images and patterns.

Letter	Identifying and recognising same/ different in size, position and number	Identifying and recognising same/ different in rotation	Identifying and recognising same/ different in laterality	Identifying and recognising same/ different in vertical inversion
K	Sorts the same letters in order of size, large to small	Identifies and matches sequences of identical shapes rotated	Identifies straight letters in correct lateral inversion	Identifies straight letters in correct vertical inversion
K	Sorts the same letters in order of size, small to large	Identifies and matches sequences of mixed shapes rotated	Identifies curved/ straight letters in correct lateral inversion	Identifies curved and straight letters in correct vertical inversion
L	Finds the same letters in different fonts	Copies and over-writes commonly mis-orientated letters correctly in isolation	Identifies curved letters in correct lateral inversion	Identifies curved letters in correct vertical inversion
L	Finds the same words in different fonts	Recognises when letters have been mis-oriented	Using two letters, identifies those correctly and incorrectly orientated laterally	Identifies digits 1 to 9 in correct vertical inversion
M	Finds the same words in the same size and font among a range of distractors	Rotates letters to match correct model	Recognises one *b* in *d* distractors	Recognises one *b* in *p* distractors
M	Finds the same words in different sizes and in different fonts among a range of distractors	Sorts *d*/*p* and 6/9	Recognises *d* in *b* distractors	Recognises *d* in *p* distractors

Suggested activities or strategies

Word hunt

Teach the child to recognise words presented in different ways.

- Word art. Explore ways of representing the same word in different styles.
- Explore computer fonts.
- Write your name, cut and paste your school's name or collage your street name in letters of different/increasing/decreasing size.
- Word search. Complete simple and increasingly complex word searches.
- Word hunt. Find given words in sentences, paragraphs and pages of favourite books. Give the child the target word in a different font or size.

Rotation continues

Teach the child to copy a range of orientations.

- Roundabout. Collect a set of five or six objects/shapes/pictures of shapes and provide a set to the child. Arrange your set in a left to right sequence. Place each item in a different rotational position (e.g. shoe facing left, shoe facing right, shoe vertical facing up, shoe diagonally left to right). The child should then use their own set to match the sequence identically one at a time.
- Rock around the clock. Draw a simple picture, for example, an umbrella. Copy this picture five or six times and place in a left to right sequence. Change the orientation of each item. Provide the child with the identical five or six pictures and encourage the child to match and paste the sequence from left to right.

Orientating letters horizontally

Teach the child to horizontally orientate a letter shape correctly.

- Sort magnetic letters from a feely bag in correct orientation. Teach the child to remove the letters from a feely bag to present to the adult in their correct orientation. To simplify this task, allow the child to look at an example of the letter to be found and its orientation. The child should not be allowed to look in the feely bag. However, it is important to be mindful that handwriting remains the most important way to discriminate.
- Create simple worksheets which contain a given letter placed randomly in its correct orientation but also contain, hidden among these letters, the same letter rotated or reflected. The child should join up all letters that are correct but ring those that are incorrect. Extend this task by giving the child a simple text to read in which there are incorrectly orientated target letters. The child should highlight these incorrectly orientated letters.
- Crossing the midline. Encourage the child to write letters/digits in front of them at a large size that crosses their midline. This will help the child understand:
  - which side the curves or straight edges of the letter fall;
  - which side the letter begins and ends;
  - how the letter is formed in relation to themselves and its spatial orientation.
- Create and laminate a simple 2×2 grid that covers an A3 sheet of paper. Encourage the child to create their letters in different coloured pens on the grid to demonstrate in which quadrant the letters begin and end and which side the curves and straight edges fall.

Orientating letters vertically

Teach the child to vertically orientate a letter or digit shape correctly.

- Use magnetic letters to create simple words. Turn one letter over so that it is incorrectly orientated. Encourage the child to notice that the letter is on its wrong side and therefore incorrectly orientated. Differentiate this task by turning over increasing numbers of letters.
- Teach the child to compre magnetic digits to identify incorrectly oriented digits in phone numbers.

Aspect 6: Visual figure ground

Letter	Locating and isolating objects	Locating and isolating parts of pictures	Locating and isolating letters and words	Saccade Control and depth perception
A	Directs gaze at groups of objects placed in a group at midline	Shares attention with adult on whole-image activity	Identifies odd letter out in a group of three	Understands concepts/ associated language of *top* and *bottom*
A	Directs gaze at groups of objects that are spaced at midline and either side of midline	Shares attention with adult on specified aspect of image/activity	Identifies odd letter out in a group of five	Understands concepts/ associated language of *middle*
B	Transitions gaze between large items in a group	Switches attention from one aspect of the image/ activity to another with prompting	Locates specific letters in a group of coloured letters	Tracks with eyes to count a range of objects (with eyes only, horizontally)
B	Transitions gaze between small items in a group	Switches attention from one aspect of the image to another independently	Locates specific letters in a group of distracting same-colour letters	Tracks with eyes to count a range of objects (with eyes only, vertically)
C	Transitions gaze between specific large items in a group of different-sized distractors	Shares attention on activity with adult, looking between adult and activity to share gaze	Locates specific magnetic letters in a group of dissimilar-shaped letters (e.g. a straight letter in a mixture of curved letters)	Tracks with eyes to follow a path left to right or top to bottom on a vertical surface
C	Transitions gaze between specific small items in a group of different-sized distractors	Follows first finger point of self or others	Locates specific magnetic letters in a group of similar-shaped letters	Tracks with eyes to follow a path left to right or top to bottom on a horizontal surface
D	Directs gaze at a specific item when similar items are at a variety of heights	Locates which half of the image the adult is looking at	Locates letters in an organised visual field of ten distractors	Tracks with eyes to follow a path with a combination of top to bottom and left to right on vertical surface
D	Directs gaze at a specific item when dissimilar items are at a variety of heights	Locates which quarter of the image the adult is looking at	Locates letter strings in a disorganised visual field of ten distractors	Tracks with eyes to follow a path with a combination of top to bottom and left to right on horizontal surface

Suggested activities or strategies

What am I looking at?

Teach the child to direct their gaze specifically. Be mindful that the child may have difficulty disengaging from the visual environment and therefore require some direction of visual attention or adjustments to the surrounding environment in order to enable them to visually isolate an object.

- What's in my hand? Encourage the child to make a simple choice from two items. Begin by holding the items, one in each hand. Move each object closer to the child as you name it. You may need to direct their visual attention by pointing at it. Work towards the child making a choice from two items placed on a small tray (or other isolating boundary). Differentiate this task by increasing the number of items in the space from which to choose and reducing the visual prompting. This activity could be achieved using a simple inset puzzle, where choices of pieces are offered to the child.

What are you looking at?

Teach the child to direct their gaze to your point, or co-ordinate it to their own.

- Play 'What's that?' The child guesses what you are looking at, and vice versa.
- Choose a picture of a simple scene. Move your finger slowly around the image for the child to follow and guess what you will stop on.
- Place items on a table and play 'Guess what I'm looking at'. The child must guess what you are looking at and you must guess what the child is looking at. Differentiate this task by:
  - gradually adding more objects;
  - placing the objects so that they are more or less spaced out;
  - arrange the objects at different heights;
  - placing some objects on the periphery;
  - placing partially obstructing obstacles;
  - using items that are larger or smaller.

Hunt the letter

Teach the child to isolate a single letter shape from a visual array.

- Letter fishing. Provide the child with a range of magnetic letters and encourage the child to fish for the letter with a magnet on the end of a piece of string. Name the letter you want the child to find while showing them a picture of the letter. Begin by using only a small number of letters and a single colour. Work towards using increasing numbers of letters and slowly increase the number of colours until there are multiple colours used. As an alternative to magnetic letters, the letters could be printed onto paper in the desired colours and a paper clip applied to each one.

Top, middle or bottom?

Teach the child to understand/use positional language and the associated concepts of *top*, *middle* and *bottom*, *under*, *below*, *above*, *in front*.

- Misfits. Play the traditional game of Misfits in which the child can mix up characters' heads (top), tummy (middle) and legs (bottom).
- Camouflage. Create artwork where you paint a creature and use collage materials to hide the creature against a background and/or behind foreground materials.
- Play games in which the child builds brick towers (e.g. Jenga®).

Teach the child to track objects moving in a variety of orientations – left to right/right to left/top to bottom/bottom to top and so on. This task can be differentiated by including increasing numbers of orientations (e.g. left to right and diagonally) but also by including increasing numbers of distracting objects.

- Marble run. Build marble runs and encourage the child to follow the marbles' path through the maze.
- Provide opportunities to count objects in a row using eyes only. Count cars in a horizontal line, or sweets and objects organised vertically (e.g. bricks in a tower).

Aspect 6: Visual figure ground

Letter	Locating and isolating objects	Locating and isolating parts of pictures	Locating and isolating letters and words	Saccade Control and depth perception
E	Locates local objects while tracking horizontally left to right	Completes a grid search (2×2, 3×3 and so on) to locate items of a single attribute (e.g. colour)	Matches like letters, digraphs and trigraphs from a field of dissimilar distractors	Completes a simple straight-edged maze
E	Locates local objects while tracking vertically top to bottom	Completes a grid search (2×2, 3×3 and so on) to locate items of more than one attribute (e.g. specific shapes of given colour)	Matches like letters, digraphs and trigraphs from a field of similar distractors	Completes simple curved-edge maze
F	Locates local items in a random group of unrelated objects	Completes a grid search (2×2, 3×3 and so on) to locate an object	Completes an organised grid search (3×3, 4×4) to locate individual letters	Completes complex straight- and curved-edge mazes
F	Locates local items in a random group of similar objects	Completes a grid search for a cluster of related items	Completes an organised grid search (4×4, 5×5 and so on) to locate digraphs/trigraphs	Completes a range of mazes containing a range of orientations
G	Locates a local specific item in an organised table top array	Completes a 2×2 grid search in an image creating a busy background for a single item	Completes an organised grid search (5×5) to locate words with dissimilar letter distractors	Tracks ahead in a simple maze to plan route
G	Locates a local specific item in a disorganised table top array	Completes a grid search up to 4×4 in an image creating a busy background for a single item	Completes an organised grid search (5×5, 6×6 and so on) to locate words with similar letter distractors	Tracks ahead in a complex maze to plan route

Suggested activities or strategies

Hide and Seek

Teach the child to locate specific objects in an organised array.

- Connect Four®. Play the Connect Four game, in which the child must organise and place their counters in strings of four to win but must also 'notice' their opponent's attempts to create strings of four counters.
- Sudoku. Play Sudoku-style games, in which the child must align items in a grid so that each item only appears once in each vertical, horizontal or diagonal line. This activity should be initially differentiated by drawing a chalk grid and using physical items before completing the task on a worksheet.

Grid search

Teach the child to identify objects in a grid using an organised visual tracking search method. Begin by just having single items in the grid. Work towards the items being drawn onto a transparent overlay and placed over a distracting background suited to the search.

- Archaeological dig. Create an archaeological dig in a sand tray with appropriate objects placed randomly in a grid constructed using string. Encourage the child to look for named items in each grid square using an organised search method, that is, top left to bottom right. Differentiate this task by increasing the number of objects in each grid square, by varying the sizes of the grid squares and by asking the child to find a specific item in the array having seen a picture of it.
- Treasure map. Prepare simple paper treasure maps with either a printed grid or acetate grid overlay and encourage the child to locate and isolate items as in the previous activity.
- Bingo and Lotto. Play these traditional games, varying the number of items in the grid.

Word searching

Teach the child to visually compare strings of letters containing up to five letters to find the odd letters out that you have added or removed, and to find these letter strings within organised field grids.

- Worksheet words. Prepare simple repeated letter strings using the copy and paste function but change one of the items to be different. For example:

  mtyb mtyb mtyb mtyb **mtb** mtyb

  or

  mtyb **mtybz** mtyb mtyb mtyb mtyb

  Differentiate this task by increasing or decreasing the number of letters/digits in the target string, or by varying the colour of letters in the string. You may also vary the complexity of the string by using letters that are obviously different and moving towards those that are of similar size and shape and therefore less easily discriminated.

- Create simple word search grids where you can hide simple digraphs/trigraphs/words. Differentiate this task by hiding strings within similar letter sizes and types.

Mazes

Teach the child to track routes and paths following a variety of orientations. Begin with straight line mazes and work towards mazes with curves and a combination of curved and straight tracks.

- Mazes. Use a variety of traditional pencil and paper mazes. If the child is unable to use the motor skill actually to follow the path, encourage them to watch as you do so and to suggest possible tracks. Differentiate with mazes that increase in complexity of orientation and width of track. They should begin as straight line mazes that track predominantly vertically or horizontally, and work towards combinations of these.
- Maze-making. Encourage the child to create mazes using wooden blocks initially and then to work towards creating Lego mazes on base boards.
- Mazes with eyes only. Provide the child with a simple printed maze and encourage the child to use their eyes to predict the route through the maze. Use an object or counter to track the maze; the adult moves the object from instructions given by the child.

83

Aspect 6: Visual figure ground

Letter	Locating and isolating objects	Locating and isolating parts of pictures	Locating and isolating letters and words	Saccade Control and depth perception
H	Locates a specific named item from the environment, given information that it is *above/below* a specific height	Identifies item in narrow, horizontally masked image strip	Locates letters in a word	Follows single item moving slowly from left to right
H	Locates a specific named item from the environment, given information that it is *left/right* of a specified position	Identifies object in narrow, vertically masked image strip	Locates consonant vowel boundary in word	Tracks to look at items that appear from left to right
I	Locates an item, given information about colour	Identifies item in quadrant of image when given clues to location	Locates digraphs in a word	Demonstrates Saccade Control to stop at a specific letter in a word
I	Locates an item, given information about shape and size	Identifies item in half of image when given clues to location	Locates trigraphs in a word	Demonstrates Saccade Control to stop at a specific word in a sentence within reading ability
J	Locates items from a simplified background	Identifies object in half of picture	Locates letters, digraphs and trigraphs in a sentence	Demonstrates Saccade Control to track a sentence within reading ability left to right
J	Locates items from a complex background	Identifies object in three-quarters of picture	Locates letters, digraphs and trigraphs on a page	Demonstrates Saccade Control to track sentences across a paragraph where text runs onto lines below

84

Suggested activities or strategies

Object hunt

Teach the child to isolate a single item from a visual array.

- Kim's Game. Play the traditional Kim's Game in which the child must identify a single item removed from or added to the tray.
- Sorting tray. Create a simple tray with a range of item groups (e.g. cars, animals, bricks). Encourage the child to find one of the groups of items. This aspect of the task can be differentiated by using groups of related items (e.g. cars, boats, planes, trains). Sets of these small items can be purchased as related groups but also in matching colours.
- Hunt the object. Practice 'spotting' items hidden among other distracting items (e.g. a specific colour of balls in a ball pool; beanbags in a bucket; specific sweets in a jar; specific Lego bricks in a pile; specific Smartie colours poured from a tube).
- Play the traditional game of I Spy. Give the child clues that narrow down the search.

Picture fractions

Teach the child to visually isolate named items from simple pictures. This task should be differentiated by the size of the viewing space; make a card mask that masks off given areas of the picture.

- Picture search. Mask off parts of illustrations and encourage the child to find items in the revealed picture.
- Use the *Where's Wally?* books by Martin Handford (Walker Books) to find the character of Wally hidden among complex backgrounds.
- Use other books that encourage the child to search for specific items that are hidden in the pictures or are used to create the picture.
- Photocopy a simple picture and cut out a small piece that shows an object. Encourage the child to find this picture part in their whole picture. This task can be differentiated by cutting out only part of an object, or a range of objects.
- Picture-making. Two pictures are each cut into halves or quarters and jumbled together.

The child sorts them and pastes the pieces to create wholes when given the original images as a guide.

Letters on a page

Teach the child to isolate individual letters and letter strings in words, sentences and paragraphs.

- What's in a name? Cut up a set of letter cards or use a set of letters that can be rearranged to make the child's name or the name of others in the group. Encourage the child to select the correct letters and construct the name.
- Provide the child with a highlighter pen. Encourage the child to highlight given letters or letter strings in increasing amounts of text.

Saccade Control

Saccade Control is the ability to move the eyes from one point to another, quickly fixating on points. Support the child in tracking across lines and between lines.

- Use a line-guide to help the child to follow the line. Counter-intuitively, you may find that the child finds more benefit with the guide placed above the reading line than below.
- Use a small card window to remove peripheral visual distraction and crowding.
- Some children benefit from coloured overlays.
- Work with the child to highlight the spaces in between words so they can 'notice' these. This should not necessarily be used as a reading text.
- Use a different coloured highlighter pen to accurately highlight the words yourself. The child should be encouraged to 'notice' that word length changes. You may combine highlighting words and spaces between words occasionally.
- When the child is supported to track left to right across the page, you may find that the child benefits more if the adult holds the child's finger as the pointing tool, rather than the adult using their own finger.

Aspect 6: Visual figure ground

Letter	Locating and isolating objects	Locating and isolating parts of pictures	Locating and isolating letters and words	Saccade Control and depth perception
K	Chooses preferred item independently	Traces over and isolates the outline of one shape in an array of three shapes	Locates word in a sentence	Places self *in front/ behind/in middle/ above/below* position; understands concepts/ associated language of *foreground/middle ground/background*
K	Chooses/isolates an item from restricted choice with directing prompt	Traces over and isolates the outline of a shape/ picture in an array of three overlapping shapes	Locates word in a paragraph	Identifies and retrieves items from *top, middle* and *bottom* of a vertical stack
L	Chooses a named item from a restricted choice of objects	Traces over and isolates object outlines in array of five or more	Locates words on a page	Identifies and retrieves item from *foreground* and/or *background* and/ or *middle ground*
L	Retrieves an item from the environment by matching it to a similar item	Traces over and isolates object outlines in overlapping array of five or more	Locates the same word in a sentence	Organises objects into *foreground, middle ground* and *background* position
M	Retrieves an item from the environment by matching it to a picture of that item	Colours three simple shapes that appear as *top, middle* or *bottom* in an illustration	Locates the same word in a paragraph	Identifies items in *top, middle, bottom, foreground, middle ground, background* position in 2D images and line drawings
M	Retrieves an item when given verbal instruction	Colours three objects that appear as *top, middle* or *bottom* in an illustration	Locates the same word on a page	Organises objects into *top/middle/bottom* position

86

Suggested activities or strategies

Treasure hunt

Teach the child to conduct a structured visual search of the physical environment.

- Hunt the Thimble. Play this traditional game, in which one child is chosen to hide the object while the other players leave the room. When the object is hidden, the other players return to search for it. This activity could be differentiated by varying the colour of the object (the brighter the colour, the more easily found) or by varying/limiting the environmental background (e.g. inside or outside).

Tracing objects

Teach the child to trace a variety of shapes that appear in isolation or overlapping to suggest depth.

- Tracing overlapping objects. Provide the child with a picture that contains a range of objects drawn in outline but overlapping one another. (There are worksheets available in, for example, *Visual Perception Skills*, LDA 2007.) Encourage the child to identify one object at a time to isolate and trace over.
- Picture tracing for near and far. Provide the child with a range of simple pictures of single items. Encourage the child to trace around the object outlines. Ensure that items in the image vary in size. Include more detail/texture, suggesting closer proximity. Encourage the child to identify which object is the closest each time.

Words on a page

Teach the child to locate items within a grid using an organised search method. Provide the child with a highlighter pen. Encourage the child to highlight given words in increasing amounts of text. Differentiate this task by adding and removing pictures within the text.

Foreground–background

Teach the child to understand and use the language of position in relation to self and other objects in the foreground, middle ground and background.

- Torches. Encourage the child to use a torch and shine it on objects that they feel are near/far/in the middle ground.
- Target practice. Provide the child with a range of hoops on the floor at a range of distances: near, middle ground and distant. Encourage the child to throw beanbags into these targets. Use a different colour for each hoop (e.g. green = near foreground, amber = middle ground and red = background/distant).
- Skittles and bowls. Play a range of these simple games in which the child has to visually track an object from the foreground to the background and vice versa.
- Skipping rope. Place a skipping rope on the floor so that one end is at the child's feet and the rope runs away from them. Encourage the child to throw a beanbag to hit the end of the rope. Gradually add lengths of rope so that the target end is further away. This task could be differentiated by using a set of four shorter, but coloured, ropes laid end-to-end running away from the child. The child could then be challenged to throw the bean bag into the first half or second half or the first and closest quarter, second, third or fourth quarter.

Teach the child to recognise and create foreground, middle ground and background in 2D.

- Far and away. Draw an object (e.g. a fish) on a piece of plain A4 paper. Draw another fish and cut it out. Place a piece of tracing paper over the A4 paper sheet so that the original fish is hazed. Now place the fish you cut out on top of the tracing paper so that the original fish can still be seen. This should make the fish on the A4 sheet appear distant. Discuss with the child how the closer an object is, the more detail you see.

Letter	Moving in space	Hand–eye	Drawing and colouring	Writing
A	Maintains head in midline position	Follows first finger point	Shows awareness of a range of mark-making tools	Makes vertical movements with finger in the air
A	Moves head from midline to left, from midline to right	Follows own first finger point	Shows awareness of writing hand and successfully grasps tool	Makes horizontal movements with finger in the air
B	Moves head to cross midline from left or right to fix gaze on an object or person	Directs gaze at objects in a variety of positions	Tracks pencil motion vertically and horizontally	Makes circular movements with finger in the air
B	Moves head to fix gaze on an object or person	Fixes gaze on object/ activity focus at midline	Tracks pencil motion across a range of orientations	Touches objects on page when requested
C	Maintains head in midline position while walking and maintains appropriate attention/ gaze	Sustains gaze on object/ activity focus	Scribbles randomly in large undefined space	Places stamper/pencil to write anywhere on page
C	Moves head from midline to left or right while walking to fix gaze on objects or people appropriately	Reaches appropriately for intended focus	Scribbles randomly in a range of defined spaces	Places stamper/pencil to write within a designated page space
D	Travels at appropriate speed	Sustains gaze on object/ activity focus at midline	Stops random scribble on request	Is able to make a single mark
D	Maintains appropriate distance from others	Transitions gaze around aspects of objects being manipulated	Stops random scribble in defined spaces	Makes multiple random marks

Suggested activities or strategies

Turning head to look

Teach the child to move their head in order to direct the gaze. Teach the child also to judge appropriate distance.

- Play Follow My Leader. Place the children in pairs and encourage each child to take turns following their partner around the space (with no obstacles). Encourage a visual measure of distance by holding an arm out in front periodically.
- Take the pupil on a 'Looking walk'. They could walk and tell you things they can see on the left or right, or both left and right. You could also give a list of items to spot on certain sides as they walk.

Looking and pointing

Teach the child to follow and use a first finger point. Teach also the ability to fix gaze on specific points, together with judging what another person is looking at.

- Place a small number of objects on a table top. Cover with a cloth. Remove the cloth for a short time so the pupil has time to look and name the objects before re-covering.
- Play 'Guess what I'm looking at' by positioning a range of objects on the table at a range of heights. They have to guess what you are looking at.
- Play the traditional game of I Spy, modelling pointing at objects as you name them.

Scribbling

Teach the child to place mark-making tools in designated spaces on the page, and to make random marks.

- Use finger painting to fill spaces by drawing fingers through space and by placing fingers accurately.
- Encourage the pupil to explore a range of mark-making tools: felt pens, pencils, brushes, sponges.
- Mark-make to musical pieces, changing direction and pattern according to the music. Alternatively, play percussion instruments. The child should begin mark-making when the music starts, make marks quickly/slowly according to the sound and stop when the sound stops.

Making patterns

Teach the child to make patterns in the air and to transfer these movements onto their page.

- Use streamer sticks to make colourful patterns in the air. Encourage the child to watch the patterns their streamer makes as they raise and lower their arms. Also encourage movements vertically, horizontally, diagonally and circling to cross the body midline.
- Make finger patterns in sand.
- Make stamper patterns. Sequence stamper patterns and fill spaces with stamper pictures.
- Provide opportunities for sponge printing.
- 'Draw' on walls with a torch beam or using a paintbrush and water.

89

Aspect 7: Visual motor integration

Letter	Moving in space	Hand–eye	Drawing and colouring	Writing
E	Slows to avoid a stationary obstacle	Tracks a ball travelling horizontally crossing the body midline	Demonstrates control to make marks horizontally left/right	Begins to mark-make on a specific point
E	Stops appropriately to avoid collision with a stationary obstacle	Tracks a ball moving vertically up and down	Demonstrates control to create vertical strokes	Can stop mark-making on a specific point
F	Changes direction to avoid a stationary obstacle	Tracks a ball moving towards and away from an individual	Demonstrates control to make marks in circular motion – clockwise	Can begin and end mark-making on separate points
F	Co-ordinates movement of head/gaze while changing direction to avoid a stationary obstacle	Retrieves ball with two hands	Demonstrates control to make marks in circular motion – anticlockwise	Can begin at point and return to point when mark-making
G	Negotiates a simple obstacle course	Rolls a large ball into a target space	Demonstrates control to make marks in a circular motion to return to starting point	Draws vertically and horizontally between two parallel straight lines
G	Negotiates classroom furniture appropriately	Rolls a range of balls into targets of decreasing size	Makes marks that cross the body midline randomly	Draws between two parallel lines to follow a curved path
H	Successfully changes direction to avoid a corner, safely turning left	Throws balls into a target space	Makes marks that cross the body midline horizontally	Over-writes vertical marks
H	Successfully changes direction to avoid a corner, safely turning right	Throws balls to another person	Makes marks that cross the body midline diagonally	Copies vertical marks

Suggested activities or strategies

Avoiding obstacles

Teach the child to move in space and to avoid stationary obstacles.

- Create simple obstacle courses, **where it is safe to do so**, in a large hall space. Begin with the obstacles spread out to create large spaces between them. Gradually decrease the space between items.
- Walk a slalom-style course between cones.
- Walk from one side of the hall to the other, avoiding coloured rubber discs.
- Pupils work in small groups. Encourage the group to stand in a small space (e.g. on a P.E. mat) and to take turns moving between peers without touching.

Tracking and retrieving

Teach the pupil to track and retrieve items in motion.

- Teach the child to toss and catch a ball themselves.
- Observe and play with marble runs.
- Create and observe train sets and a Scalextric track.
- Pop bubbles with clapping hands or poking finger.
- Follow torch beam patterns and movements.
- Play tablet games where the pupil must move a target at the foot of the screen to catch falling items or manipulate falling items.
- Hold rolling ball races down lengths of drain pipe.
- The child catches balls rolled to them, using a net.
- Play golf with a junior golf set, where balls may move slower, or use an air flow ball.
- Play bounce and catch the ball from the floor.
- Play bounce and catch the ball from the wall.

Controlling tools

Teach the child to control tools through a range of orientations. Teach the child to move to cross the midline of their body by ensuring that initially marks are large – that is, circles are large enough to move from one side of the body to the other.

- Use paint brushes and buckets of water outside (where safe!) to make a variety of marks.
- Encourage painting marks on large pieces of paper, which are lying horizontally and placed vertically.
- Chalk on outside floor areas where appropriate.
- Use stencils.

Starting and stopping to draw accurately between points

Teach the child to move a writing tool with a degree of control.

- Encourage the pupil to join two points. Differentiate by changing the size of the points and by adding other points to 'visit' on the way.
- Encourage the pupil to complete simple drawing paths between two wide parallel lines. Develop this so that lines become closer and move to change direction or curve.
- Encourage the pupil to complete simple mazes.
- Encourage the pupil to join pairs of dots horizontally/vertically and diagonally.
- Use simple dot-to-dots. Differentiate this by using mazes with increasing numbers of dots and smaller dots.

© Mark Hill 2015   *Target Ladders: Visual Perception*   LDA   Permission to photocopy

Aspect 7: Visual motor integration

Letter	Moving in space	Hand–eye	Drawing and colouring	Writing
I	Can turn to the left back to starting point	Picks up a block with dominant hand	Colour fills a space using stampers, finger paints and large sticky spots	Over-writes horizontal marks
I	Can turn to right back to starting point	Picks up and places blocks with accuracy	Colour fills a space using lines and cross-hatching	Copies horizontal marks and lines with a right-angle change of direction
J	Changes direction to avoid a moving ball	Picks up a ball with dominant hand	Colours along edge of bold outline	Overdraws incline line bottom left to top right and decline top left to bottom right
J	Co-ordinates movement of head/gaze while changing direction to avoid a moving ball	Picks up a ball and places it with accuracy	Colours to edge at right angles of bold outline	Copies incline and decline marks
K	Co-ordinates forward movement in space with a group of peers	Throws a beanbag to self and catches it	Colours multiple spaces with a variety of colours	Over-writes curved marks
K	Co-ordinates forward movement in space with a group of peers where obstacles and changes of direction are required	Throws a large ball to self and catches it	Completes a symmetrical colouring activity	Copies curved marks
L	Co-ordinates head movement to direct gaze when moving	Catches large balls	Draws to a point	Draws and closes straight-line shapes (square, triangle, diamond)
L	Moves purposefully in a range of directions and changes direction	Catches balls of a range of sizes	Draws accurately between a range of points	Draws and closes curved-line shapes (circle, oval)

Suggested activities or strategies

Avoiding moving obstacles

Teach the child to move within space to avoid moving obstacles (other people).

- Play Follow My Leader.
- Play Walking Tig or Stuck in the Mud, in which the pupil must avoid being touched by peers.
- Play a simple game of Circle Dodge Ball.

Throwing and catching

Teach the child to roll and throw balls with increasing control over increasing distances. If the pupil struggles with accuracy in this task, decrease the distance from the target, increase the target area size and use balloons, which will travel more slowly. If the pupil completes this task well, increase the difficulty by asking the peer partners to move slowly while rolling/throwing and catching.

- Play a traditional game of bowling with foam balls and skittles.
- Roll large balls into hoops placed on the floor.
- Roll large balls between partners' legs/two standing poles/a hoop held vertically.
- Throw large balls into buckets.
- Encourage the pupil to throw and catch balls with peer partners.

Colouring and drawing

Teach the child to draw and colour with increased control and detail. For children struggling to colour in the early stages, encourage the child to fill the space with lines, spots or cross-hatching.

- Try colouring within raised lines (squeeze PVA glue to make a raised outline).
- Thicken paints and encourage the pupil to push paint within the space using fingers and tools. For example, use cotton wool buds or brushes and sponges to fill spaces with spots of colour or to push paint.
- Try colouring within thickened lines.
- Encourage the use of larger colouring tools to cover the colouring area more quickly.

Tracing lines, symbols and letters

Teach the child to trace lines and simple shapes or pictures. To differentiate this activity, gradually increase the shape/picture to include curved and straight lines. Also, increase the complexity of the picture detail. Consider increasing the number of connecting shapes and the number of shapes inside shapes.

- Encourage the pupil to complete traditional tracing activities.
- Make a set of laminated mats that each show a black outline of a shape. Work with the child to roll out lengths of play dough and mould to follow the outlines to create each shape. Differentiate this task by creating regular and irregular shapes and by using straight and curved lines.

93

Aspect 7: Visual motor integration

Letter	Moving in space	Hand–eye	Drawing and colouring	Writing
M	Can move in a range of directions and change direction alongside peers	Builds a simple block tower	Completes a simple dot-to-dot with straight lines	Traces and writes *l, i, t, j, f*
M	Can co-ordinate movement with others for a specific purpose	Builds block patterns	Completes a simple dot-to-dot with straight and curved lines	Traces and writes *v, w, x, z*
N		Works at midline to string large beads	Copies and colours a single straight-edged shape	Traces and writes *h, b, k, r, m, n, p*
N		Works at midline to string beads of a variety of sizes and shapes	Copies and colours a single curved shape	Traces and writes *a, o, c, d, g, q, y, u, e, s*
O		Laces card with large hole in straight lines	Copies/colours straight and curved shapes that are connected	Over-writes and copies a word
O		Laces cards with large holes, accommodating changes of direction	Copies and colours shapes that are connected and held within other shapes	Controls ascenders and descenders when they write
P		Places counters onto spots	Plans to draw a simple recognisable shape	Controls spacing when they write
P		Positions mosaic tiles accurately	Draws a combination of recognisable and connected shapes	Writes within boxes
P		Places pegs into holes on pegboards	Adds detail to simple shapes and pictures	Writes between pegs or markers
Q		Cuts in straight lines	Copies a recognisable picture	Writes between lines
Q		Cuts in curved lines	Draws a recognisable picture from memory, with prompt	Writes sitting on lines
Q		Cuts around simple geometric shapes	Draws a recognisable picture independently from memory	

Suggested activities or strategies

Team games

Teach the child to move as part of a team. Play team games, such as basketball, netball, or Dodge Ball, but begin with fewer people and encourage the children to walk initially to slow the movement down.

Finger play

Teach the child to pick up items, move items and manipulate items with accuracy.

- Arrange blocks in patterns and build simple block towers using wooden bricks and Lego.
- Thread a variety of bead sizes (beginning with the largest) onto pipe cleaners, Wikki Stix and laces.
- Provide opportunities to weave paper strips.
- Use a selection of lacing cards. Make them using hole-punches to enlarge the holes to be laced.
- Teach the child to orientate shapes accurately in order to post them into a shape sorter.
- Play Connect Four, draughts.
- Provide regular opportunities to cut out shapes and pictures.
- Turn over coins. Place a row of ten coins, heads up, in front of the child crossing their midline. Ask the child to use their right hand to move from left to right, turning all the coins over to show 'tails'. Then use their left hand, moving right to left, to turn them back to 'heads' again.

Drawing and colouring confidently

Teach the child to colour accurately and draw with control and detail.

- Experiment with a range of colouring tools to identify the tool that is the most easily manipulated by the child. Consider weight, width and barrel shape.
- Encourage the child to copy drawings from a grid model.
- Encourage the pupil to complete increasingly complex dot-to-dots.

- Using a thick coloured marker, demonstrate to the child how to take the pen for a walk around the inside edge of the colouring shape. Teach the child how to colour carefully along the perimeter of the shape.
- Colour-code simple pictures so the pupil can 'see' the sequence of drawing. For example, outline the flagpole green = first, flag yellow = next and flag detail red = last.

Learning to reproduce letter shapes and patterns

Teach the child to reproduce recognisable and controlled letter shapes.

- Provide visual cues such as green spots to demarcate the starting point and red spots to demarcate the finishing point.
- Provide visual cues such as directional arrows.
- Use roller letters, where balls roll to indicate the direction of letter formation.
- Teach the child to form letters on surfaces with textures such as shaving foam. Cut letters from sandpaper or Velcro strips and encourage the child to track along them with their fingers.
- Use feely bags. Place the plastic letters to be taught in a feely bag. Show the child a target letter while the child searches in the bag by touch alone.
- Play Noughts and Crosses, and Boxes.
- Encourage the pupil to write letters of decreasing size (requiring increasing control) by providing a sheet with graduated boxes into which the child places the letters.
- Use RediSpace (pegged paper) and/or sensory paper.
- Use spacers for the pupil to hold between words.
- Embolden the lines on lined paper, or colour alternate line spaces.
- Colour-code alternate lines on lined paper. Use green and red.

Links to other *Target Ladders* titles

Target Ladders: Dyslexia
Kate Ruttle

Includes additional targets for:
- Visual and auditory perception and memory;
- Phonics and spelling;
- Reading comprehension and fluency.

Target Ladders: Autistic Spectrum
Louise Nelson

Includes additional targets for:
- Getting attention.

Target Ladders: Speech, Language and Communication Needs
Susan Lyon et al.

Includes additional targets for:
- Attention control.

Other useful resources from LDA

Visual Perception Skills
Mark and Katy Hill

Visual Memory Skills
Mark and Katy Hill

How to Understand and Support Children with Visual Needs
Olga Miller and Karl Wall

Visual Literacy Books 1 and 2
Jo Browning Wroe and David Lambert

Coloured reading overlays

Raised line writing paper

For more resources suitable for children with visual perception differences, visit www.ldalearning.com